THE RUNAWAY BRIDE

Jesus is returning, will He find you living for Him or running from Him?

D1416804

HEATHER LINDSEY

DEDICATION

I dedicate this book to my baby girl Lindsey who will be born in July 2015. Words cannot express how I'm looking forward to raising you to know Jesus. As I sit here, writing, I can feel your strong kicks. I know that you are going to be a strong woman that runs towards Jesus and not away from Him. I pray that you will always pursue Jesus with all of your heart and never quit on Him. He is for you and never against you. Your value is never in what this world calls popular, it's in the cross. It's in being obedient to the Lord in the midst of a world that hates Him. I don't desire that you become a preacher, doctor, lawyer or anything else. I desire for you to be obedient to the Holy Spirit and are led by Him in everything that you do. The Lord has called you with purpose long before He placed you in my womb (Jeremiah 1:5) and the beauty of learning Christ is learning what He's called you to do. So, my sweet babygirl, we look forward to meeting and training you up to know Jesus. See you soon. Hugs.

Thank you's:

To my husband, Cornelius Lindsey who constantly pushes me and inspires me to write what the Lord puts on my heart and keeps me accountable. I couldn't ask for a better husband, father to our babies, and leader over our home. You truly support me in whatever the Lord has put on my heart and I thank you sweetheart. I love you so much.

To my sweet Logan who has taught me so many life lessons in his two years of life. You made me a mother which is one of the most beautiful gifts on this earth. You fit perfectly into our family and I am forever thankful for you. I love you!

To my amazing family, your support and help is appreciated. I thank God for every single one of you.

To my Pinky Promise Dream Team, you ladies help me so much behind the scenes. Words cannot express my thankfulness. I love you all dearly!

To my Pinky Promise sisters, I will love you all forever. Thank you for always supporting me. I'm so proud of your growth and don't you ever stop living for Jesus.

TABLE OF CONTENTS

WHO IS THE BRIDE?

THE RUNAWAY BRIDE

THE INSECURE BRIDE

ARE YOU HOLDING ONTO DIMES?

GOD, I CAN'T DO THAT

INTRODUCTION

But I have this against you, that you have left your first love. **Revelation 2:4**

After I preached "The Runaway Bride" at the 2014 Pinky Promise Conference, I thought I was finished with the message. The Holy Spirit had other plans and told me that He wanted me to continue the message. As I wrote this book, I felt a great, great urgency and heard The Lord speaking into my heart, "Heather, tell them I'm coming back for my church! I'm going back for my bride! Tell them to get dressed and keep their oil full. Tell them not to get distracted, tell them to not worry for I have not forgotten about them! Tell them not to get weary in well doing because I Am returning!"

I know for years we have heard that the Lord is coming back but, I think we are now closer than ever to His return. He is cleaning out the church and truly separating and *revealing the sheep and the wolves*. He's showing who really wants Him and who **just wants status and a stage**. He's revealing hearts so that we can see the authentic and real. We live in a generation where in some states, calling homosexuality a sin is considered "hate speech" and businesses are getting fined for not supporting gay marriages. We live in a generation where living together before marriage, having sex outside of marriage seems "normal" and a prerequisite to marriage so you can "try out the car before you buy it." Women are on this "I don't need no man because I am independent" approach to life and they have totally ignored the beauty and value in being a Titus 2 woman, one who loves God, can still run a business, submit to her husband as unto the Lord, and run her household with grace. Our men are more interested in sports than they are in lying out horizontally before God and getting instructions on how to keep their family out of hell.

It seems like this generation is getting further and further away from God. And if I can be totally honest, I write this with tears in my eyes because it breaks my heart. Satan is after us and He is looking to destroy people any way that He can destroy them. He doesn't care about you! He just wants you out of the way so he can try to destroy the next person in your family.

So, this is why I wrote *The Runaway Bride*. We are generation of people that has run away from God. You may not live with a man outside of marriage, but that man lives in your mind. He is the object of your affection. You think about him to the point where he becomes an idol. You plan your day around him, he constantly rejects you and doesn't think twice about you as you center your entire life around him. Or, maybe you are celibate and you brag that you've been celibate for three years, two months and four days but you turn on pornography every single night to satisfy your lust. Or maybe you're married and you just want to run away from the responsibilities of being a wife and mother. Maybe you're just sick and tired of the day-in and day-out routines that you're thinking, I just want to RUN Lord! All the while, the Holy Spirit is telling you to **"STOP! Don't go there, don't open up that computer, put down that dish and come spend time with me. Close your school books and come and study My**

Words." We can begin walking away from God and without even realizing it, our walk turns into a full out run from Him. You see, we have to recognize that when we tell Him "No" we are moving in the opposite direction. Would you, in your wedding dress—see your groom at the end of the aisle and start running in the other direction? Of course you wouldn't. But sadly, we run from God in our dresses every single day. Turn back around love, it's time to stop running.

CHAPTER 1

WHO IS THE BRIDE?

Recognizing that you are the bride of Christ is one of the most powerful images that one could get into their hearts. "The Bride of Christ" is symbolic for the relationship between Jesus Christ and the body of believers, known as the church. In the New Testament, when Jesus came to the earth to die for our sins, he sacrificially and lovingly chose the church to be his Bride.

> *"Husbands, love your wives, as Christ loved the church and gave himself up for her, that he might sanctify her, having cleansed her by the washing of water with the word, so that he might present the church to himself in splendor, without spot or wrinkle or any such thing, that she might be holy and without blemish." **Ephesians 5:25-27 ESV***

This scripture tells us that Christ gave up His life for the church (us) so that He may sanctify the church, having cleansed her by the washing of the water of the word that He may present the church (us) without spot or wrinkle to God. Jesus had to come to the earth and die for our sins because without Him, we were destined for hell. He became the "door" to reconnect us back to God. Jesus reconciled us back to God after the sin in the garden. No other god did this and this is why we are the "bride" of Christ.

> "For your Maker is your husband, the Lord of hosts is his name; and the Holy One of Israel is your Redeemer, the God of the whole earth he is called." **Isaiah 54:5 ESV**

> "For I feel a divine jealousy for you, since I betrothed you to one husband, to present you as a pure virgin to Christ." **2 Corinthians 11:2 ESV**

If anybody on this earth was a runaway bride, it was me. When I was at my absolute worst, when I hated myself, wanted to kill myself and when I felt the lowest in my life, God picked me and choose me. He made me His own even though I was least deserving. I believe that Ezekiel 16 clearly describes my unfaithfulness to the Lord.

*Then another message came to me from the Lord:
"Son of man, confront Jerusalem with her detestable
sins. Give her this message from the Sovereign Lord:
You are nothing but a Canaanite! Your father was
an Amorite and your mother a Hittite. On the day
you were born, no one cared about you. Your
umbilical cord was not cut, and you were never
washed, rubbed with salt, and wrapped in cloth. No
one had the slightest interest in you; no one pitied
you or cared for you. On the day you were born, you
were unwanted, dumped in a field and
left to die.* **Ezekiel 16:1-5 NLT**

This was literally my story. My birth mom found out
that she was pregnant with me and went to an abortion clinic
to abort me. But, I was measuring 4.5 months and she didn't
want to abort a child that was so far along. So, although I'm
sure I was cared about in general, I wasn't wanted. I
understand that my birth mom couldn't raise me and she
made the best decision that she knew to make. To this day,
I'm thankful that God had His hand on me and He gave me a
chance to live. Don't think that I'm holding this against her. I
was put up for adoption. So, I can relate with you if you were
born and were considered a "mistake." I can relate to you if
you grew up feeling rejected, even though you were loved by
your family. I can relate to you if you grew up feeling like

nobody cared about you, even though you were surrounded with people that did care for you.

Let's keep reading:

"But I came by and saw you there, helplessly kicking about in your own blood. As you lay there, I said, 'Live!' And I helped you to thrive like a plant in the field. You grew up and became a beautiful jewel. Your breasts became full, and your body hair grew, but you were still naked. And when I passed by again, I saw that you were old enough for love. So I wrapped my cloak around you to cover your nakedness and declared my marriage vows. I made a covenant with you, says the Sovereign Lord, and you became mine.

"Then I bathed you and washed off your blood, and I rubbed fragrant oils into your skin. I gave you expensive clothing of fine linen and silk, beautifully embroidered, and sandals made of fine goatskin leather. I gave you lovely jewelry, bracelets, beautiful necklaces, a ring for your nose, earrings for your ears, and a lovely crown for your head. And so you were adorned with gold and silver. Your clothes were made of fine linen and costly fabric and were beautifully embroidered. You ate the finest foods— choice flour, honey, and olive oil—and became more beautiful than ever. You looked like a queen, and so you were! Your fame soon spread throughout the world because of your beauty. I dressed you in my splendor and perfected your beauty, says the

Sovereign Lord. **Ezekiel 16:6-14 NLT**

At this point in your life, your life has hit rock bottom. You are literally kicking in your own blood, tired of being addicted to men, pornography, chasing after money and a career that God never told you to pursue. You are depressed. You are frustrated with life. You want to quit. This is when God reveals Himself to you and says "LIVE!" He saves you and calls you His own! You walk down the aisle and give your heart to Jesus at a church service. With tears in your eyes, you recognize your need for a Savior. You recognize that no other god can fulfill you like the Lord Jesus Christ. You recognize that only Jesus died for your sins and you are ready to walk with Him. So, God begins to put you back together. He cleans you up, makes you whole, teaches you the truth, reveals the people to you that shouldn't be in your life and He provides for you. You are His bride and He pours His presence on you.

Let's keep reading:

> *"But you thought your fame and beauty were your own. So you gave yourself as a prostitute to every man who came along. Your beauty was theirs for the asking. You used the lovely things I gave you to make shrines for idols, where you played the prostitute. Unbelievable! How could such a thing*

ever happen? You took the very jewels and gold and silver ornaments I had given you and made statues of men and worshiped them. This is adultery against me! You used the beautifully embroidered clothes I gave you to dress your idols. Then you used my special oil and my incense to worship them. Imagine it! You set before them as a sacrifice the choice flour, olive oil, and honey I had given you, says the Sovereign Lord.

"Then you took your sons and daughters—the children you had borne to me—and sacrificed them to your gods. Was your prostitution not enough? Must you also slaughter my children by sacrificing them to idols? In all your years of adultery and detestable sin, you have not once remembered the days long ago when you lay naked in a field, kicking about in your own blood. **Ezekiel 16:15-22**

So at this point in your life, you start to get tested after you've been saved for a little while. You begin to think highly of yourself. You look down on other people that aren't saved but then you start to do the very things that they do, but privately because you're embarrassed. Like Adam and Eve, who hid themselves from God because they were embarrassed by their sin, **you end up doing the same exact thing.** You run back to the sin that God freed you from because you miss what you thought was comfortable. You prayed for that job and you got that job but now you cannot *stop bowing down and worshipping that job.* Worshipping my job, Heather? Now, that's a little extreme. Well, you may not admit it with your mouth but your actions prove that you worship your job. You spend 50-70 hours a week at work and you are way too busy to spend time with God. You rush to work, work all day without even thinking about God unless you send a tweet, trying to encourage others. Then, you get home from a long, exhausting day and you eat, watch some garbage TV and then, when you start to get sleepy, you jump in the shower, sit down in your bed, open your bible and read it for three minutes as you doze off to sleep. Whenever your boss tells you to do something, you drop everything and do it in fear of losing your job. But when God tells you to do something, you rationalize for a year, "praying" about it before you move. There's no rush, no urgency and no reverence for Jesus. He's an accessory in your closet that you wear but some of you aren't totally sure that He even told you to be at that job. Let's be honest, *you don't desire God because you give Him no attention, no time, no energy because you've given all of your attention to your idol.* **You want money so bad that you revolve your life around getting it instead of revolving your life around the Lord Jesus.** You've made shrines out of the things that you prayed for and it's time to burn those idols to the ground because those idols are temporary and God is jealous for you.

I have an image in my head of you walking down an aisle in a beautiful dress, giving your life to Jesus. Then, as the Lord, Jesus has his arms open, waiting for His bride you begin to turn in the other direction. Imagine being in your wedding dress, the one the Lord designed perfectly to fit you, with diamonds and gold jewels in your hair, bowing down and worshipping some man that only wants to have sex with you outside of marriage who is there for your wedding. How silly do you look? Taking off your wedding dress to give your body to a man that doesn't even care about you! He doesn't love you! Your groom is at the END of the aisle but, you got distracted on your way to Him! That man lusts you and God is trying to warn you that this guy is not your husband! He's trying to warn you that sin separates you from Him and He cannot tolerate intentional sin (1 John)! But in your head, you're thinking that you are lonely, feeling sad and you *miss having a man close to you*. What you don't know is that this guy has a sexually transmitted disease that is not curable. "But, he used to be my boyfriend, so I know he doesn't have any STD's

Heather." Well, he contracted it a week after you broke up with him the first time God told you to cut things off. And although he has a condom, it will break and your life will be shortened by 70 years for three minutes. **A condom won't protect you from a broken heart.** A condom won't protect you from a broken spirit. From soul ties, drama and in all actuality, lying down with him will make you feel even worse about *yourself.* And what you don't understand is when you do get married, you may compare your husband to all the men in your past. You may even still dream about those men and miss those men, all while you post on social media how much you love your husband as you paint the perfect picture. Honey, you have so much crap on the inside of you and if you pretend that it isn't there, it's going to seep out into your marriage. You are going to charge your husband for what those *men you should have never dated did to you in your past.* How do I know? I used to do the same exact thing. I had major trust issues when my husband and I first got married. Even though we waited to kiss until our wedding day as I shared in my first book, *Pink Lips and Empty Hearts* and all that other good stuff, I still found that all of the mess that I picked up when I dated around before him, came back up in my heart even though I thought I had buried it.

As I mentioned before, I had huge trust issues. I would give my husband the eye if he said he was going to the barbershop. Are you really going to the barbers shop? And I would call and text him the entire time he was there. You see, prior to meeting my husband and when I dated in the world, I had a few really bad, dysfunctional, physically and verbally abusive relationships. I stayed in these bad relationships and one in particular, where a man would beat me up. I didn't fight back because he was much bigger than me but I would always run back to him. I felt like him hitting me meant that he loved me. One night, as a teenager, I sat in his apartment and I balled my eyes out. **I felt like if I lost him that nobody else would want me.** I felt like my value was in him and I didn't want him to reject me. Breaking up felt so final and I was afraid so I even suggested that we get married. Thank GOD He protected me as a minor to make sure that I didn't run to the courthouse to marry that psycho man but his cheating, abuse and constant lies for three years built a few walls of hurt in my heart. Then, I continued to attract bad relationships like the one above. Although there was no physical abuse, there was a lot of cheating with the guys I dated. So, if he cheated on me, I cheated on him. I never wanted to cheat, I just wanted to get revenge which is silly because I was only hurting myself. What a waste of time! I could have spent those years as a single woman, totally pursuing God! Totally filled with His spirit! Pouring into other teens and being led by His spirit! Granted, God is using it to remind me to remind others of what NOT to do growing up.

Let's keep reading:

*"What sorrow awaits you, says the Sovereign Lord. In addition to all your other wickedness, **you** built a pagan shrine and put altars to idols in every town square. On every street corner you defiled your beauty, offering your body to every passerby in an endless stream of prostitution. Then you added lustful Egypt to your lovers, provoking my anger with your increasing promiscuity. That is why I struck you with my fist and reduced your boundaries. I handed you over to your enemies, the Philistines, and even they were shocked by your lewd conduct. You have prostituted yourself with the Assyrians, too. It seems you can never find enough new lovers! And after your prostitution there, you still were not satisfied. You added to your lovers by embracing Babylonia, the land of merchants, but you still weren't satisfied.*

"What a sick heart you have, says the Sovereign Lord, to do such things as these, acting like a shameless prostitute. You build your pagan shrines

> *on every street corner and your altars to idols in every square. In fact, you have been worse than a prostitute, so eager for sin that you have not even demanded payment. Yes, you are an adulterous wife who takes in strangers instead of her own husband. Prostitutes charge for their services—but not you! You give gifts to your lovers, bribing them to come and have sex with you. So you are the opposite of other prostitutes. You pay your lovers instead of their paying you!* **Ezekiel 16:23-34 NLT**

This is you, walking back down the aisle that you came from, in the exact opposite direction from the Lord. As you run to these other men, these things, these empty idols, I want you to imagine the Lord Jesus Christ constantly PURSUING you as you walk in the other direction, intentionally choosing other gods. He EVEN wants your crazy thoughts, your sins, your dysfunction, and your suicidal thoughts. He wants ALL of you! So, from sister to sister. STOP running. Just stop it! You've been running from God after He saved you and you live like He doesn't even exist! You get hit with problems and you stress out and try to figure out what to do. **You have more faith in your bank account than you do the only Holy God.** Your husband steps out on faith to do something and you nag and worry about bills to the point where it hinders his faith and he goes practical instead of faithful, all in the name of your worries. Then, because you've pressured him "Eve" to do something that he knows that he shouldn't be doing, sin enters your marriage and there is a repeat of the Garden of Eden in your living room.

At what point did you let the serpent into your home? Did the Holy God not tell you to trust Him? Who are you listening to and why are you entertaining the enemy's lies and then nagging your husband to do something that he shouldn't be doing to fulfill your discontentment? *When we truly live for God, we trust Him in every single area.* I'm not writing this as if I'm perfect but you better believe **that I got tested in writing this book**. There were areas that I learned I wasn't surrendered to God in and God had to come in my heart and fix that mess. You have some areas in you as well and it's time to confront those areas. In this book, we are going to take a huge flashlight and shine what's going on in your heart, bride.

In Jewish custom, it was typical to have a "betrothal period" where the bride and groom were separated until the wedding. This is symbolic because we are separated from Christ for a time period. He came to this earth, died, rose again and is in heaven, interceding for us. Then, the Lord will come back for a church (bride) that is without spot or wrinkle (Ephesians 5:27). **So, Jesus is returning to the earth to take us back with Him forever and it's like you being unfaithful to your husband the night before your wedding.** How crazy would that be for you to cheat on your fiancé right after the rehearsal dinner? Of course you wouldn't! You are too focused on sitting in your hotel room with your bridesmaids and talking about your wedding day! Your focus is on seeing your groom at the end of the aisle and joining him in covenant! It's not sleeping around with random men! You wouldn't dare do that to your fiancé, would you? Then, why do you do that to your first groom, Jesus?

It's the night before your wedding.

Where are you going? What are you doing? Why are you chasing after these temporary things on this earth?

At the second coming of Jesus Christ, we will be united with Him forever (Revelation 19:7-9). At that time, all believers will live in a city known as New Jerusalem or the "holy city" (Revelation 21:2). The Apostle John wrote the book of Revelation and he saw a city come down from heaven adorned as the "bride" of Christ. Meaning that we will live in this NEW city, redeemed of the Lord, holy and pure, wearing white garments of holiness and righteousness and live in a place where sin will NEVER tarnish it. Can you believe it? There will be no tears or pain and we will live with God for eternity. Some people have misinterpreted Revelations 21:9 to mean that the holy city is the bride but it cannot be because Jesus Christ died for His people, not the city. The city in this chapter is called the bride because it includes all who are the bride, just like students of a school are sometimes called, "the school."

As Christians, we should be in great anticipation of this glorious day! The day that our Lord will return for us! We should stay alert and live as though our groom is returning tomorrow morning! So, let's remain faithful to Him and committed to Him.

CHAPTER 2

THE RUNAWAY BRIDE

We've been running from God for way too long. And most of us don't even believe that we are running. You go to church, you're "saved" and it seems as though when He tells you to do something, you rationalize, question it, attach a scripture and then "**write YOUR vision and make it plain to YOURSELF**" without even asking God what HE wants to do. You have an entire vision board created of material things and ideas of who you think you should be but God has nothing to do with it. I once had a vision board with things on it and I look back and I am absolutely not doing a single thing on my vision board. I wanted to host television, I wanted a certain type of "look" for my future husband and all of these other material things. I did end up hosting TV at one point, but I felt so unfulfilled, so unhappy, and then I would get upset because things on my vision board weren't being fulfilled. Then, you get weary, bitter, and even mad at God and all the while He's sitting there, waiting for you to surrender yourself completely to Him. God, "when are you going to come through for ME?" Your relationship with God becomes a "gimmie, gimmie, gimmie" versus, "Lord, let thy will be done in my life."

Aren't you tired of running from God? Tired as in the physical sense because when you run from God, you run right into problems. When you take life into your own hands you come up with your own plans and ways. This probably means you took a job, got into a relationship, started a project or did something without acknowledging God. Now, you are working sixteen hours a day at a *job God never told you to start*. You're almost to partner at that job and the Lord tells you to quit the job. You cry out, "Lord! What do you mean? I cannot quit my job! I have been at this job for ten years and I'm almost a partner! Do you know how bad I've wanted this? It was on the "vision" board I made where I put "Jeremiah 1:5" and I put all of the other selfish desires of my heart, God! Then the Lord speaks to you, "My Daughter, I never told you to take that job. I never told you to even interview but, because you have hardened your heart against me you ignored me. When you went to college and you took out $100,000 in student loans to prepare for this position I interceded on your behalf. I knew that you were going to go to college without acknowledging Me and then, take this position. **You've hardened your heart against me for all of these years and I knew that one day, your heart would be open to receive instruction from Me.** That time is now. That time is here. I tried to tell you when you applied for schools that this wasn't My will for your life. I tried to tell you as you stressed out and became worried about your courses. When you stayed the night at that young man's house who didn't know me. I tried to tell you. I tried to whisper into your heart through preachers, teachers, and evangelists. **I spoke through so many people but you kept running from my instruction.** I tried to tell you not to take that apartment but because you chose to live for yourself, I interceded on your behalf and I knew the day would come where you would listen to my instructions. So, listen to my words my daughter. **I want you to let Me lead your life and guide your life.** I want you to lay all of your plans, all of your thoughts, your school, your job, your marriage, your boyfriend, your loneliness, your fear, your stresses at my feet. I want to truly fill you up but you have to stop wrestling with Me."

Sister, you have to remember that its GOD alone who started the work in you and God alone will finish it! Will you let Him start the work in you or are you too busy trying to figure out your own life that you don't have time for God?

"Being confident of this very thing, that he which hath begun a good work in you will perform it until the day of Jesus Christ." **Philippians 1:6 KJV**

We must trust the work that the Lord has started in our hearts! HE started it! So, at what point did you pick up your life and start living it, thinking that you didn't need God? You may be thinking, "Heather! Of course I need God! I go to church, I live for Him, I give offerings, I pray and I do all of these things." Ok. But have you obeyed the Lord in the last thing that He told you to do? **You cannot give part of your life to God and hold onto the other 10% of your life**. Are you a 10% Christian? You give 10% of your life; 10% of your money; 10% of your time to God and you keep the other 90% for yourself, while partially obeying the Lord? Or maybe, you're patting yourself on your back because you gave up something here and there. And, I could congratulate you for it but I know that God demands that we surrender EVERY single area of our life to Him! We cannot hold onto pieces of it and think we are truly His in our heart! I'm reminded of this story in Matthew.

Jesus called out to them, "Come, follow me, and I will show you how to fish for people!" Immediately they left their nets and followed Him. **Matthew 4:19-20**

Immediately they dropped what they were doing and they followed Jesus. They didn't ask questions, they didn't ask where they were going, they simply obeyed Jesus. Immediately.

I think some of us could learn from those disciples. I'm sure they had bills to pay, I'm sure a crazy thought popped into their head or after they left their father, he had something to say about it later. So, let's take it a little closer. *What do you do when God instructs you?* Do you immediately obey or do you call a friend, post about it on Facebook to get your 428 "pretend friends" to give an input, pray on it for four years while doing nothing, complaining about "what the Lord told you to do" as if woe is me. Why do you care what your unsaved ex has to say anyway? The list could go on and on.

THE RUNAWAY BRIDE

You'll ask everyone but the One that told you to do it. You are in disobedience because delayed obedience is still disobedience. James 4:17 says "it is a sin to know what you ought to do but not do it." So, you know what God is telling you to do but you're afraid. You don't know how things will work out and you aren't sure if it is you, God, or the devil. Well, my friend that's a problem. It's important to know the voice of the Lord so you aren't running from Him. How do you hear God's voice? I can completely relate with this question because there was a season in my life where I couldn't tell whose voice was speaking to me. Then, I began to spend time with God daily and I would hear Him instruct me to do something and I knew without a shadow of a doubt. How?

1. It always required faith. It seemed much bigger than me.
2. I'm not smart enough to come up with it.
3. Peace always accompanied what I heard.
4. It was biblical.
5. I was so convicted to DO that thing that I couldn't shake it until I obeyed God.

How would I know it was the enemy?

1. Scripture was twisted or used out of context (this is why it's important to spend time with God and know the Bible for yourself because we know that Satan is a fan of twisting some stuff.)

2. Fear typically followed his lies.

3. They were all lies such as, "you will never make it, you have no purpose, you have no worth, nobody cares about what God told you."

4. The lies played off of my past. Things like, "you remember what happened the last time you tried to step out on faith. This God stuff doesn't work, remember? You've been saved for some time now and God still hasn't come through."

5. It caused me to worry or think that God wasn't for me.

How did I know it was me?

1. If it was selfish. Hey, at times, we can look out for ourselves. For example, I went to Target and

bought a couple items. Then, as I was checking out, I heard an audible voice that said, "Give the cashier twenty dollars." Huh, Lord? Twenty dollars? I'm confused, I'm just checking out and I definitely didn't plan to give the cashier any money. Although it was a big deal to me at that time because I was really living by faith daily and had very little money, I knew that the selfish side of me wanted to keep it, but because I went through my rational: 1) Satan wouldn't tell me to give anything to anybody, 2) I wouldn't come up with it because I was planning on only buying groceries today. So, after I gave her the money, she looked down at the money when I said, "The Lord told me to give you this" and she dropped to the ground and started crying. I walked away because I didn't want her to give me credit for something that my *selfish self didn't plan on doing in the first place.* Thankfully, I was a fairly new believer and I didn't understand giving like I do now. Now, I LOVE to freely give because I know all this stuff on earth is temporary, so it's important to worship God and not money.

2. There's no way my mind was even on that thing—

it literally just popped up in my spirit.

3. If I was trying to protect myself from getting hurt.

4. I had no peace.

5. I felt rushed or like I ran ahead of God.

I would intentionally spend hours with the Holy Spirit and I would talk to Him about everything. I would wake up in the morning and say, "Good Morning Daddy!" I never wanted the Holy Spirit to feel ignored so I would ask Him if I should curl my hair or not, help me pick out my outfit or to make breakfast with me. I know that the Holy Spirit is more real than any human sitting next to me so because I knew He was with me, I didn't want to be rude. We surely wouldn't ignore someone we could physically see so I just became very intentional about including him in everything. I figured that if I was going to hear God's voice, I needed to recognize His voice. **I couldn't be skipping around here listening to everybody else's opinion, mindset, and thoughts on my life because they didn't know me before I was in my mother's womb.** I had to de-clutter from the world, social media and anything that distracted me because I wanted so bad to hear the voice of God. I realized that God was always speaking, but typically the transmission is off and it's not on His end, but our end. James 4:8 says that "when we draw close to God, He draws close to us." How amazing! God actually draws close to us! There's seven billion people on this earth and God actually wants to draw close to little ole' me. I don't know about you but that's actually humbling. I get excited about the fact that I get to connect with the Father through Jesus Christ!

I would notice the seasons in my life or the days where I didn't spend time with God. I was moody, irritated, and low on tolerance for people. I would make comments like, *"I don't like humans today or feel like being around them."* My compassion was low and I wasn't very focused on winning anybody to Christ. I learned at that point that I was running on empty. When your car needs gas, you go to the gas station. When your body signals that it's hungry, you eat food. *So when your spirit man is starved, are you filling it up with the word of God, prayer, and meditating on the Lord?* In my own life, I would just lay in bed, totally exhausted and scroll along on Facebook or check the news. What a waste of time when I could be sitting at the feet of Jesus! If Jesus was standing right next to you, you wouldn't ignore Him! You would sit down and ask Him a million questions! So, why do we ignore His very Spirit? The

Holy Spirit that lives on the inside of us leads and guides us **and is MORE real than any human sitting next to you.** My problem was that I was running around to church, to prayer, to helping people, to doing all of these "God" things but I wasn't connected to my power source, the Holy Spirit! **How can He lead and guide me throughout life if I never talk to Him?** After sitting in God's presence, He gives me perspective about life and shows me the areas that I need to work on.

If I was in a room with a million people and I heard my husband scream, "Heather" – in the midst of those voices, I would be able to spot my husband's voice because I've spent years with him 24-7. The same goes for God. When you're in the midst of your life and there are a million voices screaming out to you, when you've spent time with Him every day, you will be able to recognize His voice. Heather, how do I spend all day, every day with God? Keep your thoughts on Him. Fast and remove anything that is distracting you. When you wake up, when you go to sleep and throughout the day, talk to Him. Then, you will start hearing Him talk back to you. It's a one-step at a time journey that will teach you to trust God for daily instructions. Don't abort the process; it's so very worth it.

CHAPTER 3

THE INSECURE BRIDE

One of Satan's biggest weapons is doubt. Satan loves for us to question who we are and how we measure up to others (Ephesians 2:1-2, 6:12; 1 Samuel 16:7). He wants us to feel insecure over the meaning and purpose of our lives, about where we're going and how we'll get there. If Satan can get you to doubt God, then you don't think that He will use you. If Satan can get you to doubt your looks, you will think that God spent less time on you and more time on another. If Satan can get you to doubt your purpose, you will chase after money, get rich schemes and other things, all distracting you from your main purpose. More than anything, if Satan can get you to doubt God's love for you, you will quit on God all together.

I just exposed his plan. So now that you know, let's fight BACK.

Have you ever felt insecure before? As women, I think it's like a secret society where we pretend like we have it all together. We pretend like we are confident, we never compare our lives to anybody else, we always feel beautiful, and we always have it all together.

Let me tell you right now that it's a lie.

EVERY person on this earth has dealt with this area of insecurity.

Including me.

As you all know, I share my story of being adopted, growing up, and feeling rejected and not being good enough. I grew up in a small town where I constantly compared my looks to everybody else's looks. Social media and technology wasn't as popular, so, instead of comparing my life to a person's life on Instagram, I compared my life to my classmates. It seems like they always got the guys and no guys from my school asked me out in elementary, middle school or even high school. I went to a predominately Caucasian school and I honestly felt left out.

Well, maybe if my hair was straight enough or if I was skinnier or if I was this or that, maybe guys would like me. I measured myself by a mirror called men. If they gave me attention, I ran with it and I felt good about myself. If I walked by a group of guys and they didn't give me attention, I would go home and feel rejected. Yes, it was that deep for me. Hey, I was 15, what do you expect?

Those insecurities didn't leave me when I got to college, it only got worse. Now, I'm on a campus with 45,000 students and ALL of a sudden, men are giving me attention. I look around and think, "WHO are they looking at because there's NO way they are looking at me!" I CONSTANTLY looked at everybody else and compared my life to their lives! I just wanted to feel like I was enough. I just wanted to be enough. So, while in school my freshman year in college, I maxed out about 5 credit cards, buying clothes and makeup to make myself feel better about who I was. I figured that if I could not fix this feeling on the inside, *at least I could dress it up on the outside*. I wore all of these clothes to fill this God-sized void in my heart that could ONLY be filled by God!

How FRUSTRATING! Then, I jumped into a relationship with someone and what did I see in him?

Nothing. He was older and he gave me attention. The attention I once craved when I watched little boys flirt with little girls when I was 10 years old. The 10-year-old girl inside of me wanted so badly to feel secure in who I was so I acted out on my insecurity by dating a man that had no standards. I didn't know how I was supposed to be treated because my affection craved hurt. "If you hurt me, it's ok. I'll ride or die. I will ride and die for you because I have no standards and I don't feel good about myself. I'm afraid if you leave me, then I will be rejected and I don't like that feeling. I don't like being single because my security is in this relationship."

Thankfully, I found my way right out of that relationship and eventually gave my life to Jesus after a couple more dysfunctional, purposeless relationships.

So now, I KNOW better and not to be insecure, right? I gave my life to Jesus, He washes my rejection, hurt and pain away and now I'm all of a sudden "confident that He that started a work in me will complete it" (Philippians 1:6). Psh, I wish.

I have to be honest, I think some people from the outside looking in think that, for some reason, I have it all together. Like I don't have "ugly" moments, like I don't feel insecure in the calling of ministry, like I don't feel I'm enough. Let me clear this up really quick so that you know, you're not the only one. I have my moments where I feel absolutely not good enough, not pretty enough, like I didn't preach a sermon right, like I didn't write a blog right, like I didn't do this or that right.

I want to highlight a few areas where I noticed insecurity hitting us the most as women.

Let's look at the definition of insecure: to be insecure is to lack confidence or trust, whether in ourselves or someone else.

And to be totally honest let's call it what it is, **insecurity is OUR failure to trust God.**

> *But blessed are those who trust in the Lord and have made the Lord their hope and confidence. They are like trees planted along a riverbank, with roots that reach deep into the water. Such trees are not bothered by the heat or worried by long months of drought. Their leaves stay green, and they never stop producing fruit.* **Jeremiah 17:7-8 NLT**

When we are insecure, we are placing our CONFIDENCE and our hope in something ELSE other than

Jesus Christ. So, of course this world is wandering around here insecure. Do you know that the plastic surgery business is a BILLION dollar industry? If you don't like it, let's change it to make you more "appealing" to society.

So, the first area we are going to look at in regards to getting attacked with insecurity is our looks.

Your Looks

In a world of Photoshop, airbrush, YouTube gurus who have crazy before and after's and whatever else, it may be hard to embrace who God called you to be. As I mentioned earlier, it started out with my looks but, then it trickled into other areas where I used those areas to measure my security. Sadly, looks will fail you because they're built on a foundation called "society." You may feel like your hair isn't curly enough, or straight enough, or you aren't light enough or dark enough. You may walk into a room with other single Christians and immediately start comparing yourself to them because you feel like you're not enough. Or, a guy at church may pass you over—and you REALLY liked him and thought you guys would court God's way—for one of your friends. Don't you DARE let insecurity rob you from knowing that God hasn't forgotten about you. God knows the desires of your heart and you looking at this fine man at church but God is looking at his HEART. He's saying, "Baby girl, he may look good to you but his purpose doesn't match yours. So, I'm going to protect you from this relationship. I'm going to keep you hidden so he doesn't even look at you." YOU may be thinking it's YOU He doesn't like but it's really God BLINDING his eyes from seeing your beauty.

On TOP of God hiding you, one group of people MAY think your pretty while in another culture, they think you're unattractive. I recall meeting a family in an African country who told me that my husband was unhappy because he was skinny and I needed to feed him more. Whoa. Huh? In their country, the men and women were much larger because the larger you are, the more "prosperous" and happy you are. Huge difference from America huh?

Today, we are assured that our looks aren't everything. You can have all the looks in the world and die tomorrow. Or, you could get into an accident and lose your looks. We must settle this truth that "And those who know Your name put their trust in You, for You, O LORD, have not forsaken those who seek You" (Psalm 9:10). We must get back to our first love. Our real trust. And that's in Jesus. Our hope and our confidence is in Him, not some man's opinion of us.

Let's look at another area where we are attacked, in our "status" or materials.

Money & Possessions

I believe that the world gives us a false sense of security when it comes to things. So, if you accumulate a lot of things, you're blessed. If you don't have much, you are cursed. If you don't have the latest iPhone, newest car, biggest house, bank account or whatever else, then you're considered a failure. It's almost like whoever has the most toys wins in life and that's totally incorrect and not biblical. The Bible is clear when it tells us not to put our hope in things on this earth but in God alone. I had to go through a season where I got rid of a lot of things because I found my worth in those things. Now, I buy quality things so I don't have to buy them twice, not because my worth comes from them. I also don't hold too tight to anything because I know that at any moment God can tell me to get rid of temporary things. What a waste of time and energy to think that temporary things actually mean something? It's all vanity and a waste of time.

*Teach those who are rich in this world not to be
proud and not to trust in their money, which is so
unreliable. Their trust should be in God, who richly
gives us all we need for our enjoyment.*
1 Timothy 6:17 NLT

I can assure you that money and things will bring insecurity to those who place their hope in them.

Worrying about the Future

Another area I find that people struggle in, and even in my own life, is being worried about the future. Oh God, what if I never get married? Oh God, what if I can't graduate? Oh God, what if my husband divorces me like my dad divorced my mom? Oh God, how am I going to pay these student loans? What am I going to eat tomorrow? Lord, I don't have any money! I thought you said you would take care of me?

*"Therefore do not be anxious, saying, 'What shall we
eat?' or 'What shall we drink?' or 'What shall we
wear?' For the Gentiles seek after all these things,
and your heavenly Father knows that you need them
all. But seek first the kingdom of God and His
righteousness, and all these things will be added to
you. Therefore do not be anxious about tomorrow."*
Matthew 6:31-34

This goes back to my point earlier; insecurity in God providing for you will cause you to doubt HIS provisions! If you doubt that God will provide for you, fear will grow in your heart followed by no peace and eventually depression. You will begin to meditate on your situation or "what ifs" rather than saying, "Lord, you're faithful. I trust you. Show me what to do. Give me wisdom Lord.

Distractions of this world

Insecurity may also result from being preoccupied with the things of the world: "Do not love the world or the things in the world. If anyone loves the world, the love of the Father is not in him" (1 John 2:15). Let's be clear, security is not to be found in this world's people, things, or institutions, including government institutions. Some people become obsessed with having the right leaders in government, the right laws, and the right policies. When the government is in the wrong hands the nation is doomed. However, the Bible teaches us that God is in control and His sovereignty extends to governmental leaders (Proverbs 21:1; Daniel 2:21). While we should practice good citizenship and vote our conscience, we must also recognize that government policy cannot save us. Only God can do that (Isaiah 33:22; Psalm 143:6).

Others place their trust in their pastor or other church leaders. However, men can and will let us down. Only Christ is the sure foundation. "So this is what the Sovereign LORD says: 'See, I lay a stone in Zion, a tested stone, a precious cornerstone for a sure foundation; the one who relies on it will never be stricken with panic'" (Isaiah 28:16). Jesus is the solid rock and our only hope of security (Matthew 7:24).

Often, one of the primary reasons for our insecurities is an undue preoccupation with our own selves, an "it's all about me" mentality. The Bible warns us about self-absorption and pride (Romans 12:3). God's work will be done "'not by might nor by power, but by my Spirit,' says the LORD Almighty" (Zechariah 4:6).

True security comes when you recognize that "God will supply every need of yours according to His riches in glory in Christ Jesus" (Philippians 4:19). When struggling with feelings of insecurity, never forget God's promise: "You will keep in perfect peace those whose minds are steadfast, because they trust in you." (Isaiah 26:3).

We have to stop thinking that temporary things will fulfill us. They will leave us empty and broken. Jesus is returning for His church—one without spot or wrinkle and you can no longer afford to be caught up in the silly things of this world. This world will fail you. I said, this world will fail you, so, we must find our security in the Lord. We belong to Him and Him alone. Will you be ready for your wedding day or will you stand before God as an ashamed bride, feeling regret or will you stand before Him, humbled because you were intentional on this earth to choose Him?

CHAPTER 4

ARE YOU HOLDING ONTO DIMES?

Our one-year-old son Logan loves to get into everything and we constantly have to make sure that he isn't eating anything he isn't supposed to be eating.

When we moved into our new home, I started to unpack and Logan loves to help us out with tasks. As I was unpacking, I noticed that Logan picked up two dimes out of one of my tote bags. He held the dimes in his right and left hand as he clinched his fists. I said to Logan, "Baby, what are you going to do with those two dimes?" He started to bring his hands up to his mouth as if he was going to eat the money. "LOGAN! Are you doing the right thing? We don't eat money, we save it, give it, and we spend it. So, please put the money back in mommy's purse." Logan placed one dime in my hand. "Logan, sweetheart, what are you going to do with that dime? Can you please give it to mommy? He cut his big, brown, adorable eyes down and shook his head "no" really hard. He started to slowly lift his hand towards his mouth as if he was going to eat it. Then, he stood up and attempted to run away from me with the dime still in his hand! I quickly grabbed him and as he got upset, I pried his little hands open and took the dime away from him. He was pretty upset with me and walked away to play with his toys. As I sat there, continuing to unpack the Lord spoke to me. He said, *"I have many children that are doing the same exact thing that Logan did to you."* At first, I was confused **"What do you mean Lord?"** He continued, **"Heather, they are holding onto dimes in their hands. They give me a part of their life. They hand me one dime but secretly, they're still holding onto their lives.** They are still holding onto their job, their boyfriend, their money, their pride, their ego, their parent's wishes, their idea of who they should be, their goals, their five-year plan and whatever else they think they can't trust me with. Then, when I gently encourage them to let go of the other dime that is keeping me from fully communing with them, they get mad at me. They begin to run away from Me. They punch and kick and they get frustrated with Me. **They doubt my existence and they crown themselves as god all over a temporary dime."**

So, is that you sister? Do you hold onto pieces of your life while totally refusing to surrender your entire heart to the Lord? Are you like my one-year-old son? How silly does he look in trying to eat money and then getting mad because I took it away? Logan doesn't understand the purpose for money yet and that is why he abuses it! **And if you don't understand the purpose for the things in your life so you will end up abusing them too.** Unless God becomes your very foundation and you take every dime, quarter, dollar and lay it at HIS feet, you won't truly see the life that He has planned for you. Let me say that again, if you don't completely and totally surrender every plan, every idea, every thought, every frustration, every person at the feet of Jesus, then you won't see the plans that He truly has for you. Why? Because you're lukewarm. You have one foot in the world and one foot in His kingdom.

Revelation 3:16 tells us "But since you are like lukewarm water, neither hot nor cold, I will spit you out of my mouth!" (NLT). You see, you aren't fully persuaded that

Jesus is the only way. You still think that you can live the life that you want and still belong to Him. Sis, He requires all of you.

Matthew 10:39 says that *"If you cling to your life, you will lose it; but if you give up your life for me, you will find it"* (NLT). If we look at the definition of cling from Webster's dictionary, we see that it's to "hold on tightly to." A few synonyms are to hold on to, clutch, grip, grasp, clasp, attach oneself to, and hang on to. Some of you are still grasping some things in your life but at the same time, you still want the benefits of living for God fully surrendered!

I remember sitting in a church service with tears in my eyes next to a man who I really wanted to *marry* and hearing the Lord say: "Heather, he's not it. I need you to let this go. If you don't cut this relationship off—it will only get worse." I didn't understand why God was telling me to let go. I wanted so bad to hold on to him because he made me feel good about myself because relationship to me equaled value and worth, even if that relationship opposed God. Everyone said we looked so cute together and even though we had sex outside of marriage and even though we messed up over and over again, I repented. I didn't feel like our purposes lined up in this relationship but I was willing to sacrifice everything because I went hard for love, even if it was the wrong kind of love. I have always had this "I'm going to make it happen attitude" all of my life but the issue is, I loved hard, **I loved the wrong people and I placed those people ahead of God.** As I rationalized this relationship, I continued to hear the Holy Spirit whisper into my heart. "My Child, let it go."

So, after church, we walked out and I was a little uneasy. People at church always talk afterward, so I was talking to everyone and thinking, "You have no clue what I'm going through. You have no clue that I've made this relationship an idol. You have no clue how broken I am. Is the Lord telling you anything? I have a soul tie with this man and I can't unglue myself from him. Even though I'm a leader at church, I need prayer. I need to be free. Stop telling me that we are so cute together externally. **Internally, we are so wrong for each other and I know it.**" I tried to play off my overwhelming thoughts as we walked into a nearby restaurant. As we walked inside and sat down, I was so nervous. God, am I really going to break this off? Then, I heard these scriptures in my heart:

*"If you love me, obey my commandments. **John 14:15***

57

You must worship no other gods, for the LORD, whose very name is Jealous, is a God who is jealous about his relationship with you. **Exodus 34:14**

Don't put your trust in mere humans. They are as frail as breath. What good are they? **Isaiah 2:22**

If I really loved God, I would break things off because clearly, this relationship has turned from *"excitement to pretend love to lust to dysfunction to idolatry."* How did this happen?

1. It happened because we were never supposed to go down that path in the first place. When you get on the train that is going in the wrong direction, instead of making a bed on the train and setting up shop, you are supposed to get off that train and get on the train going in the other direction. You see, we didn't set boundaries and we gave Satan an open door in our relationship from day one because we should have never made it past "Hello." And it wasn't like I met him at a club or somewhere ungodly, I met him at church! I think that at times we assume that just because someone attends church that both parties are actually living for God,

which was far from the truth. A tree is to be identified by its fruit, not its location and we didn't have the character or the fruit to sustain that relationship.

2. It happened because as it was getting late, I didn't get my butt up and go home. I started to rationalize—we aren't going to do anything. We are only going to cuddle. Girl, please. I hadn't renewed my mind considering courting God's way, so, over time, one thing led to another. We had no boundaries and if you don't have a standard, your flesh will set one for you.

3. Let's be honest, he actually told me he was going to be a senator or some big name and he needs a wife that is doing something similar. I told him that God has called me to preach and he didn't believe me. He pretty much said that I need to get a higher degree and to become something that God didn't call me to be. He walked by sight and I walked by faith. We were unequally yoked even though he appeared to know the bible. The proof was in his fruit and it showed that he belonged to another.

4. I had no peace with him whatsoever. It was

manufactured peace. I was trying to believe this lie that everything was OK but I knew deep down it wasn't right. I knew I wasn't supposed to be with him.

5. Lastly, I didn't want to be lonely. I wanted to run from those lonely feelings that reminded me I was going to be single soon, all in the name of obeying God. I didn't want to be single, Lord! I didn't want to start all over in a relationship! I want to be successful, Lord! I was so frustrated with God because when I sat alone, I had to hear my thoughts. I had to hear that I was placing my trust in humans and "I must stop because they are as frail as breath" (Isaiah 2:22 NLT).

We broke up that very day at that small restaurant and it was incredibly hard. Ironically, God was dealing with him about breaking things off as well. I was a cause to his distraction and as much as I wanted to blame him for the entire relationship, **I played a part as well**. I didn't have to lay in the bed with him. I could have stood up for God and said, "Don't we live for God? We can't do this." So, right after we broke up, I turned around and started intentionally walking towards Jesus. I literally ran towards Him. I pursued Him with such a renewed zeal because I was sick and tired of being sick and tired. I was tired of disobeying God! I was tired of choosing others over Him! I wanted to grow in the word of God and I was tired of only drinking the milk of God's word! I guarded my heart by refusing to hang out in our group of mutual friends. I didn't text him, didn't respond to text messages, or call him when I was lonely. For some crazy reason, that relationship gave me a very strong soul tie. I needed the Lord to literally snatch and break that soul tie because I felt consumed after that relationship. I thought about him all the time, I saw his photos on Facebook with other women and thought, "Is he dating them?" or whatever else. What a waste a time! Who cares if he is dating whoever? That isn't your man! That isn't your Adam and when your Adam (Genesis 2) wakes up and finds you, He will be sure not to let you go! A godly man isn't taking that chance of losing you.

So, I spent a lot of time with God because I knew Satan was after my mindset and my own selfish desires were after my mindset. I would meditate on scriptures for hours and hours on worry, fear, trusting God and discontentment. I would fast from my TV, social media, my phone and anything else that would give Satan a door in my life. And at that point in my life, I was in about 4-5 weddings so I obviously wanted to get married and everyone around me was getting married. I had to protect my heart from words or people until I wasn't so fragile.

I've learned that when we let go of a job, a person, a thing or whatever else, God is protecting you. In Psalms 121:7 (NLT) it says that "The LORD keeps you from all harm and watches over your life." So, if God is keeping you from all harm, **then you have to stop inviting the harm into your home.** He's trying to show you that those things aren't for you! There's a fork in the road and those things and people aren't going where you're going!

I know it's hard but what other option do we have? Let's not make any more excuses of "easier said than done." Let's instead say, "God, I trust you. Lord, I need you. Lord, help me. Lord, I'm lonely. Lord, make me whole. Lord, break my heart until it breathes your heart. God, help me.

Here's another example to give you some perspective! Let me share the story and to protect their privacy we will call this couple Jessica and Thomas. Jessica and Thomas have been together for about six years. They planned on breaking up but in year three, Jessica found out that she was pregnant. They wanted to do the right thing by being together to raise a family, so Jessica and Thomas moved in together. They were without Christ so they didn't see anything wrong with living together. Then, slowly but surely, the Lord began to tug on Jessica's heart and reveal Himself to her. She began to see the error in the relationship and realized that she wanted a godly man. Dating Thomas was fun before the baby and Jesus. There were no standards and no expectations. But now, there's a standard and Thomas didn't like this newfound change. Jessica sat in our office weeping because she wanted a family man. A man that wanted to be around his family and not at work and with his friends all day and night. She wanted a husband from her boyfriend. But, he said he wasn't ready to be married, even after all of these years.

What's wrong with this picture? Jessica was trying to cling to and hold onto her man because she had a child with him. She was holding onto the dime but then the Lord began to pry that dime from her hand and show her that it's not His best.

I believe as women, at times we have this perfect image of a family in our mind. We want so bad to see it come to pass that we are willing to even lower our standards to see this perfect family become a reality. But as he sat there in counseling, he was so distant in his body language and when he did speak, he talked about wanting to be selfish. **Sir, you give up the right to be selfish when you have children because it's no longer about you!** Your child didn't ask to be born. We may think that dating and staying with that person because of this or that reason would be the right thing to do but, I want you to know that the relationship will only get worse. You will continue to speak different languages. You will continue to argue. You will continue to be unequally yoked. In spite of the mess, from this situation came a beautiful daughter who has a purpose. Now, put on your big girl pants and deal wisely with your baby's father with the help of the Holy Spirit. Start to put things in proper order which includes establishing those boundaries. He can't get rubs and feels whenever you drop your child off. There will be no make out sessions or every now and then sex. Things have to change.

If you're reading this, you may be saying to yourself,

"OK, this doesn't apply to me. My issue isn't men or a baby daddy or whatever else." But, if you're lying down and having sex outside of marriage, this COULD be your story. Prayerfully, you will read this and not want this for your life.

From woman to woman, my heart broke for Jessica. She deserves a godly husband! She deserves a good man! She was right in expecting husband-like duties from him but wrong because she wasn't married to him. The family has been attacked for so many years and its God's very idea for transforming this earth!

Consider this, even if you don't have Jessica's story do you have Jessica's mindset? It may not be a relationship that you cannot let go of, it could be school or your job. Maybe you've been at your job for six years of your life but God is trying to lead you down another path. Maybe some of you are in school to become this occupation because it's what your parents said you needed to do, or what society pushed on you because of money. If you do things for money or earthly success, you will become a slave to those things. Some of us need to go and sit before the Lord and ask Him these questions:

Lord, am I holding onto any dimes in my life? Is there

something or someone that I cannot let go of because I'm afraid? I'm afraid of being alone. I'm afraid of not having enough money. I'm afraid of what people will think of me. I'm scared Lord.

Did you know that God can work with your honesty? He already knows that you're chasing after the wrong things but, He desires for you to sit before Him and truly let HIM change you from the inside out. **Sister, it's not about you anymore.** It's about glorifying God and being obedient to what He has called us to do. **You are over here holding onto dimes when God wants to do something so powerful in your life but you refuse to let go and move to where He is waiting for you to get to!**

What scares me about holding onto dimes is the person that God is going to have to raise up to do what I *refused* to do in the body of Christ. I know that one day, I will stand before our Father and give an account for my life and the decisions I made in my life. I don't want to stand before him with a list of excuses of why I held onto dimes and I never obeyed Him. I don't want to look back in regret over my life and wish that I shoulda, coulda, woulda obeyed Him.

In my own life as a wife, I must say that I was holding

onto dimes. The love I had for my husband was conditional. His love language is acts of service and my love language is physical touch. So, I would clean up around the house and do things as if I'm waiting for a response from him telling me how great of a wife I am because I cleaned up the house. Then, he would walk in the house and say nothing while throwing his clothes on the floor. EXCUSE ME SIR! **Have you not noticed how amazing your wife is to you?** Weariness began to grow in my heart and I would think, "Why clean up after you if you aren't going to respond in the way I want you to respond?" I wanted a "cookie" of praise from my husband because I took the effort to make sure that I loved him based on his love language. I was treating love like it was 50%/50%. If you do this for me, then I will do that for you. My performance was based on the way he treated me and if he didn't treat me the way I wanted him to treat me, *then he could expect 0% from me.*

The Lord showed me that I wasn't surrendering my selfishness to Him and I placed conditions around my "for better or for worse." Gosh, what a hard pill to swallow! So, after I received that revelation, I asked the Lord to help me to love my husband unconditionally. Literally, the next day I was tested with loving him this way. We had some miscommunication about something and he was pretty upset with me. I felt like I did nothing wrong in that situation after judging myself a few hundred times. That night, we happened to have a meeting at our house with people from the church. At about 5 o'clock, I started making dinner, not just for my husband but for everyone else who was at the house. I had plans to cook my husband this special dinner and my plans can't change because we are upset with one another. I could have stayed in my room and totally ignored him and the church meeting. How dare he "do this or that or whatever else?" As I watched Logan, cooked, jumped in the meeting in between cooking, I washed the dishes, which is pretty huge for me because I HATE washing the dishes but, I was serving the Lord. I cooked because I get to serve the Lord. It's not even about my husband; everything I do is unto the Lord. Do you know, in the middle of cooking, my husband totally warmed up and started joking around with me? I was thinking, "Gosh, do I just need to cook you a home-cooked meal when you're upset?"

I'm not sharing this story to say how great of a wife I am to my husband because please understand that I'm far from perfect and I understand this truth. However, the truth of the matter was, I was waiting for my husband to do his 50% in order for me to make his dinner in the past. I would charge him for arguments and I didn't love Him as unto the Lord, I loved him as far as his mistakes and it stopped after that point. Godly, authentic, real love simply loves. It's unconditional which means that there's no conditions on my love for you. I will simply love you and keep on loving you. Stop holding back parts of your love with your loved ones. What a waste of time! This life is but a vapor and if we continually hold onto our hurts, pains, and frustrations then God will never be able to penetrate our hearts! I am pretty confident that I picked up that tendency to give conditional love while I dated as a single. I liked a guy until he made me upset and then I would break up with him. I figured I will run and break up with you before you try to hurt me. My love was based on conditions and I practiced it so much that when I got married, I charged my husband with the same thing. Thank God for His grace in every season! He shows us things while we are single, engaged, and married so we don't take any extra baggage into our relationships.

Do you see the trend? It starts on the playground in

school where we are pushed down or teased by someone and we begin to hold pieces of ourselves back from others in fear that we are going to get hurt by them! Then, by the time we are in college, we refuse to open ourselves up to anyone or get close to them in fear of getting hurt. We refuse to be transparent with others because "they don't need to know our business." I can relate because I've been there but, I think wisdom says I should share myself with those as the Holy Spirit leads me. I don't have to put my guards up because I'm going to keep out the wrong people or because I'm hurt or afraid of what others will do to me.

We all know that godly relationships are important. Who you surround yourself with will determine your very path in life. Those people who are closest to you are influencing you whether you believe it or not. I could have married any one of the guys I dated before my husband but, you better **believe I wouldn't be doing what I'm doing now**. I would most likely be working a desk job for the rest of my life because my exes encouraged safety in my career, *not walking by faith*. My husband pulled out the gifts and talents in me and challenged me to not be led by my emotions. Sadly, I ran most of my exes and I controlled them. I wouldn't submit to them because I didn't think they submitted to God so I'm pretty sure that my own rebellion would have stunted my growth. I never respected those men because they would say that they would do one thing and then demonstrate another thing. Honestly, we were all young and pretty stupid but, if I would have never surrendered those men to the Lord and sat before Him, I know for a fact that I wouldn't be in the position that I am in today. And you won't make it to where God wants you either if you choose to stay in the same situation.

Mark my words, until you let go of control over your life and truly surrender to Him, you won't walk in your purpose. It does not matter if some person screamed over your life, "This is your season to walk in your purpose." Honey, it's not your season if you're still holding onto your life. **You may need to go through a season of being stripped away from the things that made you comfortable.** You may need to go through a dry season where you lose your friends and you become dependent on the Lord. You may need to go through a season where God breaks you from your attitude. Then, by the time people scream about your "breakthrough" you will be so humbled by the season that you just went through that **you don't even care.** You know that you've been content with nothing and now you have a little temporary something. In both times, your eyes remain on the Lord and your heart remains pure.

As you walk through those seasons to accomplish your purpose, you will experience great suffering because you understand that when God calls you to do something, **it's going to cost every part of you**. You will cling to His hand and you won't quit because He has brought you so far. Then, you will look up and smile and say, "Wow, Lord. You did all of this for me? You love me so much. Thank you for loving me God and providing for me. I know you are the source for everything, so continue to mold me into your image." Which in turn, brings more tests and trials. Praying that God molds you means that you are going to be stripped of your fleshly self and God is going to mold you into His image. Those tests and trials will develop you to look more like Him. What a beautiful exchange! Sometimes we are unable to see all the blessings that God has in store for us because we are blinded by the tests and trials. We have to get past all that stuff and trust God to get us through, over, around it all to get to him. The relationship God is offering is amazing, wonderful, and better than we can even imagine, we just have to fight through to Him if we want to see it.

As you walk towards your purpose, **all of hell will be fighting against you while all of heaven is rejoicing for you.** Because we live in a fallen world, you have to expect the attacks but, even when they come against you, you smile and say, *"Lord, you're with me. You love me. There's nothing we cannot handle together in your strength. Lord, I'm so glad that I get to rejoice through tests and trials because these tests strengthen me!"*

Do you see the difference? In good times and in bad times, you worship the Lord! It no longer becomes about an event in order to be happy. It becomes about maturing into the woman God called you to be so you can accomplish what He told you to do on this earth. Eternity is on the line so it's time to stop running.

CHAPTER 5

GOD, I CAN'T DO THAT

Has God ever told you to do something but you didn't feel like you could do it because of your bank account, your schedule or maybe you felt like you had no time to accomplish that task? I don't know about you but, I have definitely felt that way before. While I was planning the second Pinky Promise Conference, fear overwhelmed my heart. I am signing these huge contracts with hotels and I am required to pay them if the rooms don't get filled or if people don't come to the event. Even though I knew the Lord told me to host the event, I felt inadequate. I questioned what He told me! "Lord, if people don't come—I'm going to be stuck paying tens of thousands of dollars for those rooms!" As I worried, the Lord quickly checked my heart. He said to me, "**Is Pinky**

Promise not MY ministry? I started it and I only use you as a manager of the organization. It's my body of Christ and not your own. At what point did you pick up this organization and try to take it from me? Do I not add to the numbers?" Then, Acts 2:47 popped up in my heart, "And each day the Lord added to their fellowship those who were being saved." (NLT). I sat there with tears rolling down my eyes. "Wait, Lord, what do you mean? I just want to please you, I'm just nervous because these businesses don't care about my faith! They just want their contract filled Lord!" He said to me, "My daughter, did I not feed over 5,000 people with five barely loaves and two fish?"

So, I pulled out my bible and I went to John 6:1-7.

*After this, Jesus crossed over to the far side of the Sea of Galilee, also known as the Sea of Tiberias. A huge crowd kept following him wherever he went, because they saw his miraculous signs as he healed the sick. Then Jesus climbed a hill and sat down with his disciples around him. (It was nearly time for the Jewish Passover celebration.) Jesus soon saw a huge crowd of people coming to look for him. Turning to Philip, he asked, **"Where can we buy bread to feed all these people?" He was testing Philip, for he already knew what he was going to do. Philip replied, "Even if we worked for months, we wouldn't have enough money to feed them!"***

This part wrecked me! Jesus already knew what He was going to do but He was testing Philips faith! Philip was a disciple that had traveled with Jesus and been with Him! Even with everything He had seen, He was focused on the financial aspect. He focused on what He had instead of what Jesus could do. He looked at the crowd and became overwhelmed. Much like how I felt when I was planning for the conference. "Lord, HOW am I going to do this?" I looked at myself and thought, "There's no way that people are going to travel in from all over the world. I'm just a small town girl from Brooklyn, Michigan. If they don't show up then I will be stuck with this huge bill!"

So, what is the impossible task in front of you? For Philip it was: "How are we going to pay for all of these people?" For you it may be "How am I going to become a speaker? How am I going to own my own business? How am I going to get free from this depression? How am I going to be content in my singleness? How am I going to pay for school when I know God told me to go? How this, how that?" And on and on.

Let's keep reading:

Then Andrew, Simon Peter's brother, spoke up.

*"There's a young boy here with five barley loaves
and two fish. But what good is that with this huge
crowd?" "Tell everyone to sit down," Jesus said. So
they all sat down on the grassy slopes. (The men
alone numbered about 5,000.) Then Jesus took the
loaves, gave thanks to God, and distributed them to
the people. Afterward he did the same with the fish.
And they all ate as much as they wanted. After
everyone was full, Jesus told his disciples, "Now
gather the leftovers, so that nothing is wasted." So
they picked up the pieces and filled twelve baskets
with scraps left by the people who had eaten from
the five barley loaves.*

*When the people saw him do this miraculous sign,
they exclaimed, "Surely, he is the Prophet we have
been expecting!" When Jesus saw that they were
ready to force him to be their king, he slipped away
into the hills by himself.* **John 6:8-15**

What a powerful story! God used a little boys' faith to
feed over 10,000 people (you can't forget about the women
and children)! What would happen if that little boy hid his
food or his family took his food for only them to eat? Instead,
he freely gave what he had and God used it**! When we offer
nothing to God, He has nothing to use**! If you shrink back and
you say, "God, I cannot do this, I cannot do that," then you
aren't giving God anything to work with! I believe that Jesus

was trying to show us *that financial resources aren't the most important ones*. So, why are you looking at your bank account and then questioning what God told you to do? Your questioning shows your heartbeat.

"Well, Heather, I need to be able to ask the Lord questions."

Yes, I get it, but at some point, those questions need to turn from questions to thankfulness.

For example, I've been married to my husband for about five years now, what if I questioned every decision that he made? I could see our first or even our second year me asking, "How are we going to do that?" Then, three, four and now five years later I continue to question him about every decision he makes. At some point, some trust should have been developed. If you've been a Christian for a while and you're still questioning everything that God does while wondering "when is your time," then, you really don't trust Him. The beautiful thing about this walk is that when you spend a lot of time with God, you begin to know what He's going to tell you to do. I sense that God wants me to do something, and I just do it. I know what He wants me to do. The Holy Spirit is my Helper and He is Love. I don't have to pray and fast for thirty days when I feel led to help someone in a certain area. I just do it. Because me and the Holy Spirit work together, He is my Helper, we are a team. There's no room for drama or rebellion because I don't want to grieve Him. I want Him to enjoy living in this temple and I long to please the Father. When Jesus died for my sins, wasn't that enough? Why try to hurt Him more and more by ignoring Him, rationalizing, questioning His every request and taking my own life back into my hands.

I decided to move forward in faith in regards to planning the conference because I knew that it wasn't about me. It was about the people on the other side of the process that God was looking to reach. I watched God provide at the conference and I was blown away by how He made sure things were taken care of. There's no situation that is too big or too small for God. He wants your loneliness, He wants your heartbreak, He wants your insecurity, and He wants those things because when you are weak, He is your strength. He places these huge voids in our hearts so that there's always a place for Him. If you're struggling with feeling like you can't step out on faith and trust God, then practice it. I've learned that if I miss God, He will find me and lead me back on the right path. Remember that God is your Father and like a good Father, He's going to show you the correct path. So, you're absolutely right. *In your own power, your own ability and your own way, you cannot do anything.* But with Christ, we can truly do all things. With Christ, we can truly be led by His Spirit.

We should no longer ask God, "How am I going to do this or that" but ask Him, "Lord, give me wisdom to accomplish the task that you have given me." Because we live in a world that says if you don't have it, go to the bank, or go ask "mama & them" what to do. Instead, the next time you run into a problem, go and lay it before the Lord and ask Him what to do!

I recall a time where I was preparing to study to speak at an event, the Lord wasn't giving me a message. I'm like, "Lord, seriously?" I felt so distracted, so cluttered and I even questioned going to the event to speak. Then, the Lord said to me, *"Stop questioning the places I told you to go, and pray your way out of this rut."*

Welp.

Thank God that He put me back in place because I immediately started praying for wisdom, the event, and the sermon. Not even ten minutes later, the Lord gave me an entire illustrative sermon. I was so blown away! Sometimes, we can get into a routine in our lives that we no longer expect or even ask of God! I just sat before Him and said, "Lord, give me a message." No sincerity, no hunger, no expectation. Maybe you're so "mature" in your walk that you've become numb to serving God. It's become just something else you do and you have to do what you have to do. There's a difference between being "familiar" with God and being "intimate" with him. When we are familiar with God we take Him for granted. We treat God like we treat our family sometimes, with little respect and as if we can do whatever we want. However, when we are intimate with God, God sees all the flaws, wrinkles, and scars. Intimacy is a risk because we lay ourselves bare and exposed. We should strive to be intimate and stop being so familiar. Until we do this we risk dishonoring and disrespecting God in our lives.

It's time to reignite that hunger and excitement back into your heart! God is constantly speaking and you surely don't have to copy someone else because God can truly do a new thing in your heart! But, will you let Him? Or, will you make excuses for the rest of your life about why you cannot be obedient to Him because of your past mistakes? I charge you today and pray that in the name of Jesus, you press past your feelings, your "who, what, where, when and why" and decide that you are going to trust God no matter what!

CHAPTER 6

GOD, I DON'T UNDERSTAND

Have you ever been in a season in your life where it seems like God interrupted your plans? Maybe you had plans to marry this godly man and he left you. Or, you're planning to graduate in less than a year and the Lord is taking you in an entirely new direction. Or, you're married and get pregnant and you didn't plan on it. Or maybe, you get fired from your job unexpectedly. Regardless of the reasons, I want you to know that God's interruptions aren't really interruptions; **they were the plans that He set aside for you.** When we get saved, we give our lives to Jesus and then we quote the popular scripture, Proverbs 3:5-6, it says, "Trust in the Lord with all thine heart; and lean not unto thine own understanding. In all thy ways acknowledge him, and he shall direct thy paths" (KJV).

You see, the Lord is directing your path! And maybe, just maybe, along the way you have been directing your own path and telling the Lord when things need to be done in your life. There was a time in my life where I wanted to have a full-time job. I was an assistant at that job for over a year working as a temporary employee. I had no benefits and I never really got paid for overtime. If I got sick (thank God the Lord kept me healthy because I didn't have insurance), I had to just pray and keep it moving. I would give the Lord deadlines to when He could do things in my life. I would tell him by the 21st, I will have a "full time job" and I would name it, claim it and TELL God what He needed to do in my life. How silly! I didn't even ask God what HE wanted to do in my life!! I automatically assumed that I knew the correct way to go based on my limited thinking. I thought that I needed the job to be whole. I thought I needed the job to have an identity. I felt like I needed the job to feel valued but, I really needed Jesus Christ.

That season in my life showed me that for so long, I sought after affirmation from so many people and things that I stopped looking at the cross. I thought that benefits and a full time job were going to be my security until things didn't work out. I prayed for the job, I had others pray for the job, I did all of these things but, I came up empty. God never opened that door for me. Was He still God? Umm, yes. Was He still an amazing Father? Of COURSE! *You see, like a good Father, He led me right away from that job after being a temporary employee for two years.* I grew so much in my faith there because I learned that I didn't need things, I needed to be patient with God and trust His timing for my life, even if I didn't understand. I learned that God may not reveal WHY things happened but He sure comforted me, provided for me, encouraged me and reminded me that one day, **He's going to absolutely blow my mind if I only trusted Him and His ways.** Although I didn't see what He was going to do in my life, my faith began to truly grow in Him by not "getting what I wanted." You see, when you aren't getting your way and you don't understand, you typically end up being much more desperate for the Lord. You cling to Him, cry out to Him and you spend more time than you would have if life was easy breezy. So, then when you get the job, are you as desperate for the Lord? Are you as dependent? I believe that the desperation that we have for the Lord reveals our hearts and how we view Him. Do you look at God like a sugar-daddy that is supposed to take care of every selfish desire? **Instead of praying for the job, the man, the car, the kid, the whatever else, pray for God's perfect will to be done in your life.** Pray that you trust God through the process, even though you don't understand. Pray that God graces you for each day and that He will make you strong in the moments where you are weary. Pray that He directs your path, even if that means closing a door in your life. Although that first test was in 2004, only a year after I gave my life to Jesus, I ran into this test again recently.

On November 14, 2014 I found out that I was pregnant with baby number two. Don't get me wrong, I am thankful that the Lord opened up my womb because I see children as a gift of the Lord. However, that wasn't a part of my plan. As a matter of fact, I explained to the Lord the time period of when I could get pregnant which was a year after Logan was born but only for that eight month time period. Granted, I'm not on birth control nor do I support it (my conviction) but I was pretty much convinced that I could control when I would get pregnant again. Also, we were starting the process of adopting and you cannot adopt if you're pregnant. The agency we are working with told me that the youngest child in the house must be 18 months old. So, the EXACT month I told the Lord that I couldn't get pregnant is the exact month I got pregnant. I told him this because I have the Pinky Promise Conference in 2015 and it would put me as due right around the time of the conference and the LAST thing I wanted was to be 36 weeks at a conference again! The Lord sure has a sense of humor because He opened up my womb right in between three of our biggest events of the year. I came to this conclusion: "Lord, you are free to interrupt my life with your plans! I have no plans even though I think I have plans." My plan is to wake up each morning and worship you with my whole heart. My plan is to surrender every aspect of my life to you and I will no longer plan children around my events. How selfish! You have opened up my womb to bring a child into this earth to solve a problem and to worship you and I'm complaining about when you do it as if I have a say so? Gosh, break my heart and help me to focus on heaven and not this silly earth!

As I have shared before, I grew up in the country and my mother was a homemaker to 24 children! Where did I pick up that mindset? I picked it up when I lived in New York City. I saw so many people putting family and marriage aside to focus on their careers that *I subconsciously* began to do the same thing. So, I ask you, "Where did you pick up your mindset along the way?" You may have not lived in New York City but maybe you live in a small town where all they talk about is "when are you getting married?" Or maybe your family is pressuring you to get more education but you sense the Holy Spirit leading you in another direction. Regardless of the reason, we all need to really lay it all out on the table and say, "Lord, here's my life. I really surrender all to you! **I'm not just going to sing the song, I'm going to actually live this thing and I know it's not going to be easy but I trust you and your interruptions."** The amazing thing is it was never an interruption. The breakup, the loss of job, the whatever else, it was ALL a part of God's plan! At times, we can get so set in our ways and "writing the vision and making it plain" that it becomes OUR plan and OUR vision and we don't include God in it at all. Instead, we tag a scripture to whatever we came up with and God has to confuse the language of your boss, co-workers, business partners or whoever else because you're going in the wrong direction!

I'm reminded of this story in Genesis 11:1-9 (NKJV):

The Tower of Babel

Now the whole earth had one language and one speech. And it came to pass, as they journeyed from the east, that they found a plain in the land of Shinar, and they dwelt there. Then they said to one another, "Come, let us make bricks and bake them thoroughly." They had brick for stone, and they had asphalt for mortar. And they said, "Come, let us build ourselves a city, and a tower whose top is in the heavens; let us make a name for ourselves, lest we be scattered abroad over the face of the whole earth."

But the Lord came down to see the city and the tower which the sons of men had built. And the Lord said, "Indeed the people are one and they all have one language, and this is what they begin to do; now nothing that they propose to do will be withheld from them. Come, let Us go down and there confuse their language, that they may not understand one another's speech." So the Lord scattered them abroad from there over the face of all the earth, and they ceased building the city. Therefore its name is called Babel, because there the Lord confused the language of all the earth; and from there the Lord scattered them abroad over the face of all the earth.

A bunch of people got together and had a bright idea that they were going to build a city all the way to heaven. And if you check out verse 4, they wanted to make "**a name for**

themselves." The tower wasn't about bringing glory to God. The tower wasn't about telling people about God; it was about getting the glory for it to show it off. So, God had to come down and confuse their languages because He had no part in what they were doing. *Sometimes we need to ask ourselves, "What towers am I building in my life?"* What are you building in your heart that you aren't willing to shut down if God told you to quit the whole thing? I think it's a good heart-check to just ask ourselves those questions:

1. If God told me to leave my job, would I leave it? Or is my heart in it?

2. If God told me to break up with my boyfriend that is pushing me away from Him... would I really do it?

3. If God told me to go into my closet and sell what I have and give it to the poor... would I do it?

4. If God told me to give of my time when I don't feel like I have any left over... would I make time for Him?

5. If God told me to cut off a bad friend, would I do it?

6. If God told me to submit to my husband as unto the

Lord, even though I don't think he deserves it... will I do it?

7. If God tells me to put down the donut, cookies, start exercising and become healthier... would I really do it and stick to it?

8. If God tells me to dress more modest, will I ignore Him or will I really do it?

9. If God tells me to save more, do I listen or do I still emotionally spend when I'm having a rough day?

10. If God tells me move, would I move or would I come up with a marketing plan to why I cannot obey Him?

At times, we don't even realize that we've built towers in our lives that we refuse to let God tear down. We are afraid of the unknown so we tell God "NO" while screaming, "The Lord doesn't talk to me and I don't hear His voice!" **You can hear God's voice; you just reject it every time He speaks to you.** If you aren't open to hearing God's voice it's most likely because

1. You don't trust Him.

2. Maybe you've felt like you have stepped out on faith before and nothing happened.

3. You have no faith.

4. You are controlling and you like to lead your life.

5. You like your sin and you aren't ready to let go of it.

Now, I know this is very direct and a hard truth, but we won't get to the root of why we don't trust God with our lives if *we keep sugar coating it*. It's time to face the truth that you aren't ready to totally surrender your life to Jesus. You should FEAR not being obedient to the Lord. And this isn't some scare tactic. One day you will open up your eyes in either heaven or hell and the last thing you want is to stand before God and say, **"I didn't really trust you or live for you and I'm sorry, I loved my job more than you, I loved money more than you, I loved my life more than I loved you."** *Sis, there are no second chances after you die.* So, while we are here and talking, it's time to put the book down and go get on your face before the Lord. Repent for trying to hold onto your life! Repent for ignoring Him! Repent for choosing your own way! Tell God that you don't want to live without Him! Tell Him that you need help! He can work with you finally being honest with yourself.

Now that you've gone before Him and laid down your life, get prepared to go through some tests. These tests are going to peel off the layers of the things that aren't like Him in you. It's going to be a painful and at *times frustrating process.* You are going to want to quit. You are going to want to give up and you are going to want to run back to what seems comfortable. 1 Peter 1:7 (NLT) tells us that *"these trials will show that your faith is genuine. It is being tested as fire tests and purifies gold--though your faith is far more precious than mere gold. So when your faith remains strong through many trials, it will bring you much praise and glory and honor on the day when Jesus Christ is revealed to the whole world."*

One day, you will look up and the blinds will be taken off your eyes because you believed the truth and then you stepped out on faith and obeyed God. You will understand why God didn't want you with that man, or at that job, or being friends with a certain person. One day, it will all make sense. But, when you are in the midst of it, it's so hard to see what God is trying to do in your life and you truly won't see it until you take that leap of faith. As you mature through the tests and trials what used to bother you will no longer bother you. When people talk about you, it won't sting like it used to sting. Instead, you will feel compassion for those broken souls who gossip about you. When people reject you, it won't crush your whole world, instead, you will trust that God surrounds you with the right people. When you lose a job, it's not the end of the world because you know that God is your Provider! You see, this is what tests and trials do! They develop your faith and make you strong! We have to stop running from tests as though being developed is a bad thing. God uses them to pull out the things that are in you that aren't like Him.

CHAPTER 7

THE BATTLE FOR PERFECTION

I think at times in our life we run from God because we don't think that we can achieve or arrive to this idea of perfection.

At times, I struggle with the woman I desire to be and then I see myself in my current state and I feel like that becoming that woman is not attainable. Have you ever felt that way? I sure have! Even now, it's a daily renewing of my mind to let GO of this perfectionist attitude and accept who God called me to be. For me, the idea of a perfect woman is one who is disciplined. She wakes up early, makes breakfast before dawn and has it perfectly set out for her family. She prays, cleans, is super organized, works out, is dressed and her hair is combed by 8AM, her house is organized and it looks like Pinterest. She works hard at home or at a business and she manages to go to school as well. She studies when she feels like sleeping, she is very thoughtful, never forgets a birthday or to mail out her Christmas cards. She has amazing relationships, her kids are brilliant, speak multiple languages and of course, get all A's because she homeschools them. She does all of this with a smile and has no fear of the future as she obeys the Lord in everything that she does.

I don't know about you, but just writing that stressed me out! I have learned that this perfect woman that has it all together 24-7 doesn't exist anywhere **but in my head**. So, I would beat myself up as I laid in the bed at 7AM, going over my to-do list and everything that I needed to tackle. I felt like a bad wife and mother for just lying down for those extra few moments. I would put all of this unnecessary pressure on myself to achieve the ideal of this woman who was in my head and with all of my striving, something always fell short.

Then, one day, I made a decision that I was going to stop beating myself up and condemning myself. I asked the Lord for grace and wisdom on what to do that day and if that meant that I left a few dishes in the sink, then it wasn't the end of the world. "Lord, if you want me to organize my room today, show me. If you want me to finish this project, make it clear to me. God, I know I cannot do everything so I'm not going to even allow myself to get stressed out over my to-do list!"

At times, we become the runaway bride in our own home because we are running away from the responsibilities of our home. So, to deal with the pressure of not being perfect, we retreat inward. **We aren't excited about spending time with God because it becomes something else to do on our checklist.** We don't even have a desire to do things on our to-do list because the list seems so huge! I don't know about you, but if I feel overwhelmed, then I don't want to do anything but sit and procrastinate. Maybe, online window shop here, or maybe I will scroll through Instagram for thirty minutes and waste more time! It's almost like I would rather do ANYTHING but what I know I need to do because once again, I'm putting unnecessary pressure on myself! THEN, I get tested. Why? I put my shield down because I am overwhelmed by life. I'm no longer "alert" nor am I paying attention to what is going on in my life. I'm simply distracted.

"Stay Alert! Watch out for your great enemy, the

devil. He prowls round like a roaring lion. Looking for someone to devour. Stand firm against him and be strong in your faith. Remember that your Christian brothers and sisters all over the world are going through the same kind of suffering you are."
1 Peter 5:8 NLT

I think it's interesting that Peter was led by the Lord to use the example of a roaring lion. If you think about lions, they typically attack the sick, young, straggling animals. Not those animals that are strong and unbothered by its attack. Lions choose the weak as victims whether they are alone or not. This scripture is telling us to watch for Satan when we are suffering or being persecuted by this world. If you are feeling alone, weak, helpless, cut off from other believers, depressed, or frustrated. Maybe you're experiencing a new season in your life like marriage, childbirth or divorce—whatever the reason, you may be so focused on your troubles that you forget to watch out for danger. You've let your guard down because that test or attack seemed so huge and it drained all of your energy. These are the moments where you are the most vulnerable to the attacks of the enemy! Satan is prowling and roaring around this earth, looking for someone to devour. Someone who is weak; someone who is down; someone who is discontent; someone who thinks that their life before Christ was better than it is with Christ; someone who is frustrated with life. *During these times of suffering, it's vital that you grab ahold of the word of God and never let go of it.* It's not the time to play around and lower your shield of faith! It's the time to spend even more time with God. God is showing you that you need to depend on HIM and Him alone to get through these tests and trials.

In James 4:7 it says to resist the devil and he will flee from you. And if you don't feel like you have the strength, then remember that Jesus says that He is your strength when you are weak. (2 Corinthians 1:29) So, reject the idea that God is just too busy for you and isn't interested in your small problems. **He is interested in every single detail of your life.** Stop feeling like you have to figure out this life outside of Him! Let me go in my own backyard on this one. This used to be me and to this day, I have to struggle to make sure that I am not hardening my heart against God in the midst of attacks. We have to remember that God is the only One who can get us out of the messes in our life. He's the only One who can help us! He's the only One who can give us wisdom when we are lost. He's the only One who can lead our lives when they feel hopeless! So stop turning against our Lord. It's not

His fault sis. Man hurt you, God didn't do that! At times, we cry out to God and we say, "GOD!!! Why did you let so-and-so die? God, why did you let this or that happen?" If I can be honest, you may never know. But instead of trying to question what you cannot change, hold tight to the One who has your days numbered. All of us have numbered days on this earth and because we live in a fallen world, where the enemy "roars around like a lion" we WILL go through things. But one thing we can be assured of is that GOD will be with us along the way. That He will help us, comfort us and be with us until the very end. We don't have to be afraid of the things that are going on in this earth. We GET to trust God and His ways! He gave us sixty-six books in the beautiful Bible giving you instructions. It's like they're love letters from God to us, *saying that you're not alone, I am with you, so stop worrying.*

I used to think that God was like a man. I couldn't totally trust Him because I felt like He was going to hurt me as a single woman. So, I would give bits and pieces of myself to God and still hold onto the relationship area. I still needed to hold onto that 10% of my life because I was scared that God was going to make me marry somebody that I didn't want to be with or wasn't attracted to. I was scared. My dad was a great father, awesome provider and great husband but he passed when I was 17 years old and I never got a chance to get to know him as a man. I think now, we would get along very well but, when I was a teenager, I hated life and everyone. So, because my dad and me weren't super close, I had a STRING of dysfunctional relationships. I didn't have a standard of how I should be treated as a woman. I didn't know about godly standards, I only knew hurt. Then, year after year I continued to attract more bad boys. I gave God the side-eye as if he was like my abusive ex-boyfriend. I felt like I couldn't totally trust Him. Until one day the Lord challenged my heart. He said,

"Heather, you don't really want a relationship with me. You want what you think I can give you. You like the idea of heaven, you like the idea of having a purpose but you still hold onto your life."

Lord, wait, I go to church, I serve in five ministries, and I live for you God! My boyfriend is saved! What do you mean?"

"I told you that your boyfriend isn't my best for you and you do not trust Me. If you don't break things off, they will only get worse. I am jealous for you Heather."

I began to weep in that moment **because I realized that I didn't love God.** I pretended like I loved Him because when He told me to do something, I didn't do it. I rationalized. I mean, my man is saved, what's wrong with this relationship?

I learned in this moment that just because I was single didn't mean that I should be available to every man that came my way. I was absolutely in a relationship and that is with Jesus Christ. **This relationship never ends, even after marriage and when I leave this earth.** You see, Satan was roaring around like a lion and attacked me with another bad relationship because I was lonely. He sent exactly what I thought I wanted in a man. My type was dysfunction because I was a hot mess. I liked the challenge and the drama at that time in my life. So, he sent a Ricco-suave that looked exactly how I thought I wanted my husband to look. It was a counterfeit! What a waste of three years of my life! I was only with the man for six months and the other two and a half years, I had to deal with the soul ties and garbage that came from that dysfunction! I finally shut it all down and broke things off. I dug into the Word of God and I got a revelation of the love of Jesus! I needed to study out that word "love" because I didn't feel loved. And it wasn't anybody's fault because my family loved me growing up, it was because I was trying to cling to false love while God was trying to embed His love into my heart.

How amazing is it that Jesus came down to this earth to die for our sins and then He rose again and went to heaven and sits next to God the Father, interceding on your behalf! Jesus didn't just come to save you, **but He came to be WITH you throughout the journey so that you will enjoy eternity with Him!** He doesn't leave us alone. He gave us the sweet Holy Spirit that convicts, comforts, and leads our lives! Praise God!! Just thinking about that makes me so excited. Not only did Jesus save us but, then He gave us the answers to the open book test by placing God's very Spirit inside believers! You are NEVER alone in this walk with Him. So, if you're feeling alone it is most likely *because you've been ignoring the company that is living on the inside of you!*

How would you feel if I picked you up from the airport, ignored you when you tried to talk to me, then we got your house and I ignored you until Sunday at church. Then, at church, you try to speak to me again and I only listen to bits and pieces of what you say because of the clutter in my life? I cannot hear your voice. This is exactly what happens with the Holy Spirit! You are the driver in the example! You are rushing around and you're constantly busy and some of us only talk to Him on Sunday. You are much too busy for God because He is no longer a priority. You would never post "**God is no longer my priority because my job and my man is**" on Facebook because that's being too honest. This goes for married folks as well. Your husband isn't your God honey. Only God can fill every void in your heart. If you are single and you are thinking that a man is going to make you happy, **I want to tell you that it's all a lie.** It's an illusion and if you don't have a close relationship with Jesus, then you are going to get married and find out that you need JESUS to *figure out that man that He made.*

When we first got married, my fantasyland crumbled. I thought that everything was going to be perfect, just like the movies. We were going to skip off in the wind and I was going to be this perfect wife that always had dinner ready, in a cute dress and a smile. The house was going to be clean every minute of the day and my husband would rave about me being so perfect. I got so busy serving my husband that I forgot to serve Jesus and get filled up with Him daily. Then my nerves started to run thin with my husband. "How dare He not acknowledge that I washed those dishes?" You see, when you're spending that time with God, your nerves will thicken and what used to make you mad, won't make you mad anymore. So, make sure that regardless of what season you are experiencing in your life right now, that you are consistent in worshipping and acknowledging God.

CHAPTER 8

WHO DO YOU BELONG TO?

You may be thinking, who do I belong to really? "I know who I belong to! I belong to the Lord Jesus! I got saved when I was 12 years old and I said the prayer of salvation Heather." It's true, we all belong to something or someone but for some of us, it's just not God. From a sister to another sister, we may attend a bunch of conferences every Saturday and serve as an usher on Sunday **but activity doesn't mean that you belong to Christ.** Your life decisions are showing who you belong to! *You cannot pick up and put down Jesus as you choose!* You cannot live how you want Monday through Friday and then pick Him back up on the weekend.

When I got married, I took on the identity of Cornelius

Lindsey and I changed my last name to his last name. My old last name, Canter, no longer exists. I was happy because "Canter" needed to die. That was my old, single self and I didn't want to hang out with her any longer. In the same way, when we get saved and give our life to Jesus we take on His identity. We take on His likeness, mindset, heart and name. The old person is gone and through Christ Jesus, we are re-named. So, it's not enough to get saved and keep your old identity. Something must change, there must be a difference in your walk, your talk, your attitude, your heart.

As I was in my prayer time, the Lord showed me this huge army and in the vision, we were all marching together. I began to study the military and about those who enlist in the armed forces. I found that there's a set rules and regulations that you must live by. You cannot just pack up your bags and go on vacation whenever you want to or go wherever you feel like going. You signed a contract to literally give your life as a service to the United States of America. During this time, one has to submit to their commander and their official commander and chief is the President of the United States. When you see a solider, you automatically know that he serves this country. His fatigues identify him as one who serves. And thank God for that service! I don't know what we would do without the military that literally gives their lives to protect this beautiful country.

I realized that there are many similarities between being in the military and Christianity. Thank God that the Lord gave us free will to choose which military we will enlist in. We can either choose the army of the Lord or we can choose to join Satan's army. When we get saved, we give our life away forever and we take on the image of Christ. We join the covenant with Jesus Christ that says, because of my sins, I was separated from God forever. Then, Jesus came to the earth and He died for my sins and if I believe in Him by faith, then I will be saved and spend eternity with Him forever. So, from that moment on, we submit to and report to our new commander and Chief, the Holy Spirit who is deposited on the inside of us when we give our life to Jesus.

And, just like the army, if you choose to rebel, go AWOL or run away from the army, there's judgment. When we run back to the sin that we were saved from and continue in our sin, there's judgment. There's a separation from God. Just like an athlete running a race—there are rules and regulations that we must abide by in order to stay qualified in the race! So, as a Christian, the Holy Spirit gives us direction and convicts us of our sin to say, "Red flag on the play! If you indulge in that lifestyle and reject God, you will be disqualified!" Our "army" uniform is the Holy Spirit who lives in us! The way that you see someone in the military in their uniform is the way that we should see you, Christian when we meet you. There must be a light about you. There must be patience about you. A hope in your eyes that the world doesn't have because you belong to our King Jesus! When people meet you, do they know whose army you're in? Let's bring it a little closer, does your family or those you live with know whose army you are a part of? It's easy to pretend with strangers but it's hard to live with someone and pretend live for God. The Holy Spirit identifies that we belong in the army of the Lord. The fruits of His spirit should be living in you!

So, if you are constantly cursing everybody out that makes you upset, arguing with everyone to get your point across (and that doesn't work either), impatient with everyone you come in contact with, bitter, angry, mad at everyone and everything it shows that the fruit on your tree has yet to be burned off. That burning off process won't feel too good because God is going to have to go into our heart and uproot that old mindset. He has to go into your heart and begin to show you who you really are so that you can give those areas to Him.

So, help me understand why is it that as a society, we view a military contract as more serious or intense then our covenant with God? Some of us treat that covenant, that precious relationship with God as though it's common or optional. The Bible is not optional. It's not a pick-and-choose what I'm going to obey kind of thing.

Why is it that we are still even questioning or struggling with simple things that the Bible made clear to us? Like, "wives, submit to your husbands as onto the Lord." "Well, Heather, I am not going to submit to that man, he doesn't deserve to be submitted to with his sorry self." Ok, sister, this was the same man you prayed for and were absolutely convinced that you were supposed to spend your life with him, right? "Your Adam" woke up from his sleep and you were once so excited! What happened? Oh, the tests and trials came your way and they're pushing you around and you're too busy staring at this world that you are unwilling to soften your heart towards your husband? Or, "Let me go to my little boyfriend's house and I better pack a bag because it's already late." **Wait, what are you doing?** Why are you going to your man's house late at night? Why are you packing a bag? The Bible says to "flee fornication!" Not run to it and indulge in it! He doesn't belong to you and you don't belong to him because he hasn't committed to you in marriage. God will give you a way out of tempting situations but if you keep intentionally putting yourself in those compromising places, then soon the Holy Spirits voice will be drowned out by your emotions and feelings. **Soon, you will no longer be able to hear God's voice because you're so busy listening to the clutter around you.**

The Bible also says to stay away from the appearance of evil! So, why are you even putting yourself in a position that looks like you're doing something that you have no business doing as a Christian woman? You're in the army of the Lord and you are out here in a civilian's bedroom! "Wait, Heather—my man ain't no civilian, he goes to my church." Ah, even better. He pretends to wear the fatigue but his life's decisions prove that he belongs to another? So, are you counterfeits together? Mark my word, you want to be able to respect your one-day husband and submit to him. Many women have a hard time respecting their husbands because while they were "dating" he was more focused on studying her body than studying the Bible. You miss out on an entire opportunity to learn how to develop emotionally with your spouse if you spent more time trying to have sex than communicate. Sex isn't everything honey. It's far from it. And if you get married and you cannot figure out how to get up off of your back and communicate with your spouse then there won't be much sex going on because you will be so busy fighting one another.

And I'm not just blaming him, you have a part to play sister-girl. Don't think I'm coming hard on you either. Please hear my heart when I'm talking to you as a sister in Christ. A sister that wants so badly to see the will of God accomplished in your life but you're wasting time, energy, and money chasing down relationships that bare no fruit. Some of those men in your current life or past life should have never made it past hello but, here you are spending four and five years with this person that obviously lives for another and not Jesus.

And hear me out, living in the army of the Lord doesn't mean that you are perfect. But, it does mean that you intentionally pursue righteousness, holiness, and peace. It means that you are repentant and actually feel bad about the sin you committed. If you are making it a point to live your own life, you simply don't belong to Him. (1 John) **I feel like I have to tell you this because you've grown comfortable in your rebellion and sin.** You are comfortable with going to church on Sunday after cussing your husband out in the car. You are comfortable with sleeping around with random men as a single. You are comfortable in getting drunk after work on Friday nights. You are comfortable in your lust. It's time to truly change and surrender everything to the Lord.

"When is it my time Heather? You're married, you cannot possibly understand what I'm going through." **Well, I had to be single at one point in order to get married.** And why do we always shoot the messenger with excuses instead of actually listening to the advice? So, let me ask you, solider of the Lord Jesus Christ: How many sermons do you need to hear, blogs and books do you need to read to know that when it's God's timing He is going to bust open a door that no man can close! There are seasons under the sun for everything and it's just not your season yet! At some point, we must go from understanding the milk of that word to the meat of the word that says, "God, I am content in You and I trust You. Even if that means that I don't meet my one-day husband for the next ten years, I know that this life isn't a sum total of a diamond on my left hand's ring finger. Let me stop worshipping that idol, buy my own diamond ring and wear it as a purity band until you bring your best. You see, you need this time to prepare yourself so when your one-day husband comes around, you will be prepared and equipped to serve him. "Wait, did you just say serve him? He better serve me!" See, you're not ready to get married if you aren't ready to serve that man. Marriage is ministry. Ministry means servant. You get to serve your spouse. "But what if he doesn't serve me back?" Doesn't matter, you do it as unto the Lord, not as unto your spouse.

"Oh God, when am I going to be rich? When am I going to be a millionaire for your sake Lord?" For God's sake or your sake? Because for some reason He cannot get you to let go of that $2.50 in your purse and it seems like every time He instructs you in giving you give Him excuses to why you are the boss and the leader of your own life. So, what are your motives for being a millionaire, love? Is it for your own selfish good or is it because you truly want to help people? You want to build orphanages. You want to help the poor. You want to give more. If this is true, then you won't even think about asking God to be a millionaire. "Wait, Heather—I need to confess that thing to see it come to pass." Ok, from me to you, "I'm a car. I'm a car. I confess that in the name of Jesus, I am a car." Welp, looks like I'm still a human. You see, you cannot go around confessing a bunch of empty words. You won't see those things come to pass anyway! It's a bunch of empty words because you are looking at God to be your genie in the bottle!

We think we can use God and pick Him up as needed and put Him back down when we are done. We are confessing to be debt free but we continue to spend like crazy, we have no discipline, we cannot even make it to work on time and you are talking about you want to be rich. Money only amplifies the real you. It amplifies your need for greed and that a million dollars will never satisfy you. **You will be onto the next million, chasing an illusion.** So if you are selfish, mean, and refuse to give as God leads you when you're broke, you're going to be selfish, mean, and refuse to give as God leads you with money because you think that money belongs to you. The thing is, everything on this earth belongs to God anyway, so why are you picking and choosing if you are going to obey Him? When He instructs you and you ignore Him, *you reveal the true motive of your heart.* That you don't really want Him, you want what He can give you. It's BEST that you remain broke for a season so you can learn to manage your money and be obedient to God when He leads you. Why do I say this? Because I used to be so broke that I would go to the grocery store *by faith.* I would have just a few dollars on me to buy toilet paper but I really wanted to buy food. It was in those moments where true joy was birthed. It wasn't birthed now that I got a few books out, it was birthed when I had nothing. God *stripped everything away from me to show me that He was all I needed anyway.* I thought I needed all of these things in order to be comfortable or happy but it was all an **illusion**. I needed a close, intimate relationship with God. I clung to Him and learned that I should never hold too tight to anything on this earth because it's all temporary. So, as I walked around in my only pair of shoes, I cringed when it rained because I had a hole in the bottom of my left shoe and the water used to seep in and soak my foot. But I remembered that if God wanted me to have another pair of shoes that *He will provide all of my needs according to HIS riches and glory.* So, to this day, I don't sit before the Lord and give

Him my laundry list of things He needs to give me, like money and temporary things. I sit before Him and say,

"Lord, help me. Search me inside because I cannot live without your presence. I need You every second of every minute of every day. I cannot live without You Holy Spirit. You've done so much for me Lord and I'm so thankful for my family, my portion and I don't take it lightly. How can I be a better servant to my family and those around me? I surrender my dreams, my hopes, my goals to you God because I know that I am absolutely nothing without you. Give me a burning desire for your kingdom. Remove anything in my heart that isn't like you Jesus. I want all of you."

You see the difference? It's no longer about "Gimmie God. Gimmie." Instead, it's about, "Change me Holy Spirit. Break my heart for the things that break your heart." This is true maturity. And be careful for desiring to be rich all of the sudden. You may bow down and worship it and "In fact, it is easier for a camel to go through the eye of a needle than for a rich person to enter the Kingdom of God!" (Mark 10:25- NLT). I've been with and I've been without and I have learned to be content in both seasons.

And lastly for my examples, "God, when am I going to

be happy? I just finally want to be happy. It's not about a bunch of things, Lord. I just want to be happy." Did you know that happiness is based on a feeling and joy is birthed from who you know? When you have a relationship with Jesus Christ and you KNOW He has your back, you wake up with JOY. And if you wake up lacking joy, you stir yourself up in the Lord until you remember that all this mess here on this earth is temporary and these tests and trials are preparing you to look more like Jesus. I like to sing worship music when I sense Satan trying to attack me. We have to stop looking to events and our circumstances to find joy. How long will you hang out with the civilians and take on their mindset concerning these simple things? And if you are a new believer than it may be wise to pull away and only spend time with unbelievers when you can control the environment, like you inviting them to church or to your Pinky Promise small group bible study. You must stop drawing on your own strength in this life! You aren't strong enough to figure out your life, that is why Jesus sent the Holy Spirit to dwell in us. He is with us. He leads us. He gives us strength when we are weary. He fulfills us. He makes us whole! Our hope, our joy, our strength comes from Him alone.

THE RUNAWAY BRIDE

I remember praying and asking the Lord as a single for joy. I wanted to be happy regardless of my circumstances. And guess what happened? You guessed it, I got tested like crazy. The first fun test was when some leaders in the church made up a really bad rumor about me at church and passed the rumor around! So, all of the pastors "aids" that were men were saying some really mean things about me and smiled in my face. My guess is that the rumor went around for two months before it actually got back to me. It was so bad that I had to sit down with the senior pastor (who was pretty much untouchable so it was a big deal) and I was so shocked! How DARE they talk about me and make up such terrible rumors! This is stuff I dealt with in the world; and I did not want to deal with that drama as a believer! I thought the church was supposed to be a place of healing for me, not a place where new hurts and pains were birthed. As I shared with the pastor that the rumor wasn't true, I walked away from his office and thought, "Gosh, Lord. I'm being tested right now on being free from people bondage and still having joy in the midst of this frustrating situation. Instead of getting mad at those men." I went right to bible study that day and I lifted my hands up and worshipped my Lord Jesus! *Those mere men aren't going to throw me off my rocker!* Those men aren't going to harden my heart! **I'm going to fight back with forgiveness.** So I forgave every last one of them immediately. When I saw them, they would put their heads down in shame and I would speak up and say hello. It seemed like the enemy wanted me to crawl into a hole and hold tight to his lies. I knew those men were being used by the enemy and I wasn't going to entertain his lies. I serve the great Commander and Chief, Jesus Christ, who created everything and He is with me and not against me! He will help me. So, in that moment of choosing to give forgiveness, I passed that test.

Another similar church story happened when some of the women in the women's ministry were becoming distant. We were a small group of women so I could sense that something was going on. The Lord showed me that there was some talking behind my back and I wasn't quite sure what to do about it. So, I prayed about it and the Lord told me to purchase their shirts for the women's conference because I was over the wardrobe section and the ladies were required to give me the money for their shirts so we could all look the same. Instead, I bought the shirts and sowed into them. Then, all the sudden, the ladies were nice and kind to me. I'm not going to speculate or even wonder why because nothing was brought to me but I knew that I had to be obedient to the Lord regardless of how I felt. I've learned that when you give people things that gossip about you, it convicts them.

So, what do you do when you're getting tested? If we say we belong to the Lord, we must start responding the way that He does! We can no longer entertain meaningless things!

I could go on and on about the tests that came my way but, I don't wear them as bruises so I can brag and say "Oh, woe is me, they were so mean to me." No, I forgave them, **learned from the test and moved on**. I don't have time to focus on my past and neither do you! It's time to start learning from your experiences and stop throwing yourself a daily pity party. Nobody likes to be around people that complain 24/7 about how hard they have it in life. I'm not trying to discredit the fact that you have probably been through some really hard things but I want to encourage you to leave those things behind you. In Christ, "anyone who belongs to Christ has become a new person. The old life is gone; a new life has begun!" (2 Corinthians 5:17- NLT).

Now, the only time I look behind me is so I can rejoice on how far God has brought me and tell people where I came

from! So, cheers to submitting your life to your Commander and Chief, King Jesus, and no longer questioning the things that He has instructed you to do. No longer ignoring His tugging's to remove unhealthy relationships. No longer walking around with a chip on your shoulder as if everybody owes you something.

CHAPTER 9

LORD, HELP ME WITH MY ATTITUDE

From a woman to a woman, I can relate to those times of the month or even pregnancy when you feel like you get a free pass to have an attitude. You know, it's your hormones. You have an absolute right to crave what you want, do what you want and treat people how you want to treat them because you "just don't feel like dealing with humans." Or, maybe the attitude problem that you run into is a daily thing, where the day cannot go by without complaining about everything. You wake up, it's raining outside so you complain about it raining and how the humidity is going to ruin your hair. Then, you complain about traffic on your way to work.

THE RUNAWAY BRIDE

When you get to work, you spill coffee on your skirt and you cannot seem to get it out. Then, it seems like every single day, one thing after the next, your boyfriend, your husband, your kids, your church, your job and everything else drives you up the wall.

In the most loving way, it's not everybody else, sis. It's you.

Yikes, right? If everybody drives you up the wall every single day then there's a deeper-rooted issue in your heart. There's a foundation in your life of only being happy conditionally. Meaning that a happy event has to happen in your life in order for you to be happy. Your happiness is based in emotions and feelings and it's not based in God's word. It's not produced from joy. You just figure if your husband made more money, or if you were out of debt, or if you were skinnier or if you were this or that, you would happy. Know that even if those things happen, you will still find something to complain about because nothing is ever good enough for you and you better believe everybody else feels it around you.

Instead of complaining about the rain, wake up and say, "Lord! You gave me a brand new day to worship you with my Heart! I thank you for the rain! The earth needed the rain to produce healthy foods! I thank you that seasons change and that there's a time under the sun for everything."

As you hop in your car, you come across traffic. Well, "Lord, I am thankful that I have a car so I can get caught in traffic. There's so many people waiting for the bus in the rain and you made a way for me to have a car that actually runs. Thank you for that Lord."

You get to your job and you spill coffee on your skirt. Well, "Lord, I have a job. There's so many people that are searching for a job, so I am thankful for my portion, even though I spilled coffee that I knew I shouldn't have started drinking on my skirt. It's just clothes. **I refuse to let a piece of fabric ruin my entire day. "**

You will never, ever find true joy in Christ if you don't literally grab ahold of our thoughts and tell those thoughts that they are going to submit to the Holy God! You have to almost fight with those thoughts sometimes and tell your flesh that it cannot win! **Do you even fight back anymore or is it just, "in your head, out of your mouth"—no filter.** No saying, "Lord help me"—just a messy attitude.

As a woman, we set the tones in our home. And if you're the only one in your home then you set the tone in your home to be frustration. And if you aren't careful, you will marry with an expectation that your future husband is supposed to make you happy. **Then you will quickly find out that he is a ball of dust and that your joy cannot be dependent on other people, it must come from a deeper place**. It must come from our foundation in Jesus Christ!

So, now that we understand the symptoms of our attitude, let's discuss the foundation of why you feel the way that you do. Some of us have given our lives to Jesus and we keep getting tested, over and over again and instead of rejoicing in the midst of the test, we throw ourselves pity parties. *We create an entire marketing plan based on our hearts and we convince others to feel sorry for us.* Then, we walk around with sad faces, hoping and wishing that things will get better while we wait for the next "event" in our lives. Or, if you've had a rough past and you feel this way, then it's important to understand that only Jesus Christ came, tore the veil in the temple so that you may be connected to God again. You don't have to carry around your past and let it keep crippling you. It's just not worth it! If you are struggling in this area, go before the Lord and lay out every single day until HE fixes your attitude.

This journey is pretty hard and at times, you will feel like quitting because you're sick and tired of even trying when things aren't changing. I personally don't know why things aren't getting better but I do know that you can change one of the common denominators in the equation and that is you. It's you. Yes, I'm sure the people around you need to change but you cannot change them. You cannot change your husband's lack of leadership. You cannot change your children. You cannot change your parents. You cannot change your friends. You cannot change your boss. But what you can do is pray.

Prayer? "Heather, I need more of the deeper things of God! I went to a conference and I heard from a Prophetess and she went to the third realm of the spirit and gave me a formula to change my husband and I am going to do it."

Honey, that sounds like witchcraft, manipulation and control. You cannot change your husband, so let's settle that thing right now. It's the job of the Holy Spirit to change those around you. It's your job to pray, be patient and to trust in the Lord. I think sometimes as women, we can be such fixers. If we see an issue, we think we have the response to solve the problem and everybody around us better listen to our instructions!

And please, stop running to weird conferences where people are prophet-lying into your life and confusing you. I once attended a small conference and this woman stood up there and called me out and said that me and my then boyfriend were supposed to be married. Married? *Honey, I'm trying to break up with him but he won't leave me alone. That is NOT God, that's your flesh.* Thank GOD I didn't marry that man!

Use this time when you feel broken and frustrated to go before the Lord and mature and grow in your faith! In the hardest moments of my life, I learned to trust God when I didn't understand and I wouldn't trade those broken years for anything. So, I challenge you to start enjoying these seasons where you feel like you're getting attacked. Find something to be thankful for! Find something to be grateful for! The Lord always tells me in the midst of those rough seasons to "stop questioning and to pray my way out of this rut." I think that at times, we get weary and we forget to pray. We forget to press in. We forget to fast. It's not that we don't know to do these things, it's just that our situation seems bigger than us. Bigger than God. I believe that one of the biggest attacks from Satan is to "blow up" our problems and make them appear bigger than what they really are. Once you're in the situation, it seems overwhelming but, if we could do what Jesus said to do in those moments like to, "Give all your worries and cares to God, for he cares about you." (1 Peter 5:7- NLT) Then, we may start passing these tests and actually physically starting to feel better about ourselves. Did you know that when we pray to the Lord, endorphins are released and when you get up from prayer you actually FEEL better? Those endorphins are what make you feel good! But, if Satan can get you to think that it's all a "waste of time to pray," you won't pray. Then happy endorphins aren't released, your perspective isn't changed, your situation seems bigger than you, you won't know what to do and then you will take life into your hands and respond based on your feelings and not what God is telling you to do.

CHAPTER 10

FEELING FAR FROM GOD

Last weekend, I went on a little getaway with my husband for a couple days. We took a road trip a few hours away from Georgia to have alone time. To say that I missed my 1-year-old son, Logan, would be an understatement. When we packed up our car, we said our goodbyes to Logan. We knew he was in good hands but, the idea of being apart for two days made me so sad. I told my husband that I didn't want to leave him so I rushed back inside and I asked Logan's sitter if she wanted to travel with us and we could book them a separate hotel room. Her response, "Heather, he is fine. Go! You guys need alone time. Enjoy yourselves."

So, I left feeling convicted because I knew I needed

alone time with my husband but at the same time, I missed Logan. I thought about him the entire trip, FaceTimed him often, was sent videos, text messages and phone calls updating me on his every move.

When I returned two days later, (Logan did great by the way)—I was in prayer and I thought to myself, "If I felt that way about Logan and we were apart for only 48 hours, I wonder how God feels when we stray from Him and ignore Him for days, weeks, months and years?" If you're feeling far from God, you got in the car and drove away from Him, You moved, and He's still standing right there. If Jesus Himself was in a room sitting on the couch, you wouldn't go about your day without acknowledging Him. *You would cancel your plans in total awe that Jesus Himself was sitting in your living room.* You would ask Him a million questions, try to take a selfie (admit it) and you would call your friends over and tell them that Jesus Himself came to visit you. Well, you have the Holy Spirit. God's very Spirit living in you, which is the same exact thing. I believe that the Lord placed it on my heart to write this chapter and say, **God misses you.**

Yes, you. It's time for you to return back to Him with all of your heart. It's not enough to just go to church on

Sunday, Wednesday and sing in the choir. Your external actions don't make up for an internal relationship with Jesus. Being busy about being busy doesn't mean that you're in obedience. Some of you have gotten in your car and driven hours and days away from God and now it's time to turn your car around and go back to the path that you are supposed to be on. Typically, if you feel like God is silent, you may give up in your heart all together. This happens when you're getting tested and you may be tempted to get mad at God.

I know I have definitely gone through this rough season. I dated a guy that from day one, God told me not to date. But to me, he was like the perfect package. He was handsome, had a great job, went to my church, kinda sorta loved Jesus but, pretended like he did in the beginning and we would have cute kids. Hey, I'm just being honest. *It seemed like out of nowhere he started to ignore me.* **My text messages were going unanswered and so were my prayers.** I prayed and I prayed that things would work out and I told God that I was going to try and do everything right to make the relationship work but that door kept getting slammed in my face. I couldn't find a job and I was just plain frustrated. At that time, I served in multiple ministries at church and I found it difficult to concentrate on the love right in front of me. The love of and from God, my great friends and those around me at church. I started to feel like God didn't want me to be happy and He wanted me to be miserable. Even though it seemed like God was silent, I still felt like I knew He was near to me. *Despite my frustrations and loneliness, the Lord was showing me that His presence is not based on my good or bad* emotions.

At times, we want to "feel" God. The truth is, we won't always have happy emotions. We won't always feel like loving. We won't always feel like pressing forward but, we can move into our daily journey by remembering that *"Be sure of this: I am with you always, even to the end of the age"* – (Matthew 28:20 NLT) In those moments where you feel empty or like you've driven miles away from God, we have to remember this powerful promise, *"When you go through deep waters, I will be with you. When you go through rivers of difficulty, you will not drown"* (Isaiah 43:2 NLT). So, you may feel frustrated with God because things aren't going your way and you may have fallen into depression. It's time for you to get back in the car and go back home to our King Jesus. All of your flesh is going to fight you to find something more comfortable but, you must learn to train your flesh to do what the Bible says to do in the midst of tests. Here are a few things that I did when I was fell into this trap.

1. Pursue God like crazy. Remember "The Little Engine that Could?" It's a classic children's book that talks about a train that needs to get to the other side of the mountain but, couldn't find an engine to take the train to the other side. I love the book because it highlights an area that is so important to believers and that is to be determined and not give up even when things get hard. Be determined to stay in prayer, read your bible and to worship God even if it looks like nobody is going to support you. It's important that you schedule your day first with the Lord. I like to spend time with Him first thing in the morning and then I like to write out my schedule for the day and prioritize it. I always do this at the end of my quiet time so then I really believe that I'm being led by the Lord with my schedule. If I can be totally honest, there are times where I had to press, especially in the

beginning of my walk to spend time with God daily. I would fall asleep in my quiet time, get bored, distracted or whatever else. I had to be intentional about getting to this place because I knew God was meeting me there. I needed Him to fill me up. I needed His leading. I needed His guiding. You cannot expect to be a powerful Christian if you aren't connected to your power source.

2. I would get out of my house! I would plan picnics with God, pack a lunch and sit outside with Him. I would also plan outings with my godly sister-friends. I believe that there's just something about getting some fresh air and getting away from your house to clear your mind. Go for a walk, go people watch, pull away from the situation to refocus.

3. When I was getting tested I knew that the enemy was trying to get me to quit. So I was intentional about making sure that I was listening to worship music 24-7, prayer, and listening to sermons on my iPod. (I know, I'm aging myself.) I also wrote scriptures down on notecards and I would meditate on them and meditate on them every

time my loneliness started to speak to me. I actually have 10 scriptures that I like to "go to" in the midst of a test. Write these down and keep them nearby as the Lord leads you.

*I can do all things through Christ
who strengthens me.*
Philippians 4:13

*Have I not commanded you? Be strong and
courageous. Do not be frightened, and do not be
dismayed, for the LORD your God is with you
wherever you go.*
Joshua 1:9

*Be strong and courageous. Do not fear or be in dread
of them, for it is the LORD your God who goes with
you. He will not leave you or forsake you.*
Deuteronomy 31:6

*Finally, be strong in the Lord and in the
strength of his might.*
Ephesians 6:10

*The LORD is my strength and my shield; in him my
heart trusts, and I am helped; my heart exults, and
with my song I give thanks to him.*
Psalm 28:7

I will go in the strength of the Lord GOD; I will

make mention of Your righteousness, of Yours only.
Psalm 71:16

But they who wait for the LORD shall renew their strength; they shall mount up with wings like eagles; they shall run and not be weary; they shall walk and not faint.
Isaiah 40:31

Do you not know that those who run in a race all run, but one receives the prize? Run in such a way that you may obtain it.
I Corinthians 9:24

Therefore, since we are surrounded by so great a cloud of witnesses, let us also lay aside every weight, and sin which clings so closely, and let us run with endurance the race that is set before us...
Hebrews 12:1

Not by might, nor by power, but by my Spirit, says the LORD of hosts.
Zechariah 4:6

For God gave us a spirit not of fear but of power and love and self-control.
2 Timothy 1:7

It is God who arms me with strength, and makes my way perfect.
Psalm 18:32

4. I would play dress up. I know that may sound crazy and it sounds crazy to me now since I'm so busy! But when I was single, I would go into my closet and try on and put together cute outfits, watch YouTube videos and learn to do my makeup and my hair. When you are broke and you want to feel like a girly girl again, it seemed to do the trick! It took away my desire for wanting to shop because I could shop in my closet. Now, I wish I had the time to play dress up but I'm definitely thankful for this present season.

5. I surrounded myself with believers and I reached out to those who had less than I had. It's hard to wallow in your own problems when you are at a homeless shelter, serving food a few days a week. It puts life into perspective and it takes the focus off of you. Sometimes, you just need perspective that things could be a lot worse in your life. There is always someone, somewhere that would love your portion.

I have learned that just because I'm feeling a certain

way, doesn't mean that God has abandoned me.

Yes, you.

In the world of social media, technology and TV, it's so easy to *glamorize* what everybody else is doing while thinking, **"Lord, have you forgotten about me? Have you abandoned me?"**

No, God hasn't abandoned you. But, He is disciplining you. And you have a choice. You can either press through this test and mature in your walk with Him or stay the same and continue to go around that mountain as you run from God. The Israelites complained and went around the same mountain for 40 years! I don't want to look up at 40, 50, or 60 years old and still be dealing with the same weaknesses and struggles.

I'm going to scream this from the rooftop and I want you to get this: **God is MUCH more concerned about your eternity THAN He is you being happy.** Let's post this everywhere as a reminder that God isn't our sugar daddy, waiting to drop whatever we want out of the sky. Wait, did you just say that God doesn't want me happy? What do you mean Heather?

No. He wants you Holy. Holiness means to be set apart for proper use. God has to UPROOT some things that are INSIDE of you to show you that you cannot **DWELL with Him and DWELL with this world.** You are going to either hate one or love to other (Matthew 6:24). Some of the things that you think would make you happy, God actually hates. Maybe, it would make you "happy" to have sex outside of marriage. Maybe, it would make you happy to get drunk and go to clubs. You see, happiness is relative and is based on the condition of your heart. And let's just be honest, most people love the sin they are supposed to hate and **end up hating God and loving this world. They hate God because they feel like:**

"God, why did you let my mother die?"

"God, why did you let me get abused growing up?"

"God, why didn't you protect me?"

"God, why am I homeless?"

"God, why does my husband treat me like this?"

Why? Because we live in a fallen world that is plagued by sin and because sin is running rampant in this earth. But, these tests and trails we experience will prepare us if we respond in a godly way.

*"Consider it pure joy, my brothers, whenever you
face trials of many kinds, because you know that the
testing of your faith develops perseverance.
Perseverance must finish its work so that you may
be mature and complete, not lacking anything."*
James 1:2-4

*"Not only so, but we also rejoice in our sufferings,
because we know that suffering produces
perseverance; 4 perseverance, character; and
character, hope. 5 And hope does not disappoint us,
because God has poured out his love into our hearts
by the Holy Spirit, whom he has given us."*
Romans 5:3-5

The question is, what do you do with your mother passing away? Do you carry on her legacy and do what she cannot do anymore? Which is share Jesus with others? Yes, grieve. Yes, have your moments, just don't stay there. Your family member that has passed on wouldn't want you to isolate yourself and go into depression. You know your mother or that family member would want you to get up and do what God has called you to do!

What do you do about getting abused growing up? Have you forgiven the one who has abused you? I cannot imagine what you've gone through over the years carrying that pain but, don't you dare give another day or a moment to that person that abused you. You've already given them too many years. Instead, take your care to the Lord and ask Him to heal you. Ask Him to help you. Tell Him that you're upset, scared and it's hard to have relationships. He can heal you and then, He will use you to help other people that have gone through the same thing. **I've learned that my heartaches and victories are to be shared so that people may come into the knowledge of Jesus Christ** so that they may know how God took this absolutely messed up country girl from Brooklyn, MI and gave her purpose when she felt like she didn't have any. I share my pitfalls, my heartbreaks, my dysfunction, my crazy, the heartache from my past to remind others that if God can use me, He can pretty much use anyone who is willing. If you feel like you are not good enough, know that you are not—in your own power. The only One that makes us enough is Jesus Christ. He died so what through Him, you would be more than enough. So, keep your eyes fixed on Him and Him alone.

Maybe you feel like, "God, why didn't you protect me?" Honestly, I don't know what happened in your life and situation but I do know that at times, we take our own path. We make our own way and we reject God. So, while God is urging us to go in another direction, we turn and go the other way. When we do this, we reject His covering and protection.

Maybe you're homeless or you cannot find a job. Maybe money is your issue. I must say that I can relate with you. I've had my own eviction notice when I first moved to NYC after college. I cried out to God and I told Him that I was going to quit on this whole God thing if He didn't come through for me. I had been in the midst of the same test for four months straight and I was tired! He literally came through the next day and I was able to move in with a female friend and we eventually got a 2-bedroom apartment and lived together for five years before I got married. In those moments of hardship, I learned to cling to the Lord. **I wouldn't trade a second of those years of eating only eggs for dinner every night.** I began to depend on the Lord for my daily bread. I began to cling to Him for direction and clarity. You see, if I was eating 5 course meals every day and my lights were on, *I wouldn't have been as desperate for God at that point in my life.* I needed to be stripped of my mindset that money took care me. No, God takes care of me. So, if I have to sleep in my car, God still takes care of me. And things didn't all the sudden "turn around" for another three years but I went through that season of being financially tested because God needed me to KNOW without a shadow of a DOUBT that HE was GOD and GOD alone. I actually needed to be broke so I could learn how to budget $0.50 before God could trust me with anything else. God needed to SHOW me that money wasn't my god, HE was my Provider alone. I didn't truly believe it at that time, even though I sang the songs at church and served in ministry. That was my God-encounter that changed my heart forever.

Maybe you're in a marriage and you aren't happy. Maybe you want out and you feel like God cannot raise your dead marriage. If you're bored and in what you think is a dull marriage, **then most likely your relationship with God has become dull as well.** There's no way that you can honestly pursue Him with your whole heart, surrendering pride, egos, your feelings and what you think you deserve and still leave your husband. I know, I know, I may not understand your situation. But I have been in a place where I wanted to leave my husband. I actually had it planned out in my head of where I was going to go and what I was going to do. *I thought* *life would be easier without him and I was sick and tired of being sick and tired.* I believe that God designs the marriage covenant relationship to provide real love and fulfillment and the grass on the other side of the lawn is an illusion of temporary happiness.

So what if I'm not happy Heather? As I mentioned before, **happiness is relative, based on your feelings and what you can see.** You won't be happy at times in your marriage. *In marriage, you will always need to work on things.* Instead of focusing on what your spouse needs to do, ask the Lord to show you yourself and what you can do differently. **GREAT joy has been birthed in my marriage from loving my husband when I don't think he deserves it.** *Now, I actually think he deserves it because I love him as unto the Lord, and not as unto my husband.* My love is for Jesus. That's why I love my husband so hard. The love I have for Christ POURS out into my marriage. My husband has a very strong command-man type of personality and I've learned to make appeals to him in a respectful loving way. I watch the way I say things and I work on never nagging him. And, I've watched him in return love me like Christ loved the church. He even loves me in those moments that I don't "deserve" either but we've learned to push past our feelings and unconditionally love one another.

Maybe you are single and you feel like God has forgotten about you. Sis, it's nothing to God to bring your spouse to you. But do you want a spouse more than you want a relationship with Him? **Anything that you build higher in your heart than God can be used against you**. God won't share His glory with anybody else and He desires ALL of you. Not a part of you. Maybe, just maybe, this season is preparing you to show you that God isn't finished with your single season. Don't prolong this season stepping out of His timing and rushing to get a man to fill your voids. You will get a man and send him back because of he was an Ishmael and not an Isaac.

Now, there are so many scriptures that can be applied to waiting and trusting in Gods timing. Write down a couple of these and stare at them when you get tested. Stop giving into the enemy and not making this word a priority!

Ecclesiastes 3 (NLT)

A Time for Everything
3:1 For everything there is a season,
a time for every activity under heaven.

2 A time to be born and a time to die.
A time to plant and a time to harvest.
3 A time to kill and a time to heal.
A time to tear down and a time to build up.
4 A time to cry and a time to laugh.
A time to grieve and a time to dance.
5 A time to scatter stones and a time
to gather stones.
A time to embrace and a time to turn away.
6 A time to search and a time to quit searching.
A time to keep and a time to throw away.
7 A time to tear and a time to mend.
A time to be quiet and a time to speak.
8 A time to love and a time to hate.
A time for war and a time for peace.

Now, add a few words that speak to your current situation. Make this personal to you. Here are a couple of the things I have added in my own life.

A TIME to get married. A TIME to have kids.

*Add whatever "time" you see and how it applies to your life.

"For I know the plans I have for you," says the Lord.
"They are plans for good and not for disaster, to give
you a future and a hope." Jeremiah 29:11

I truly believe that God is using this time to discipline

you right now in this season. Discipline means to teach and to train. Discipline sounds negative to many people because some disciplinarians don't seem very loving. God, however is the source of all love. He doesn't punish us because He enjoys inflicting pain but because **He is deeply concerned about your development!** He knows that in order to become the person He has called you to be, we must learn the difference between right and wrong. God's LOVING discipline enables us to do that because He leads and guides us to the right path and way.

YOU are NOT alone in your tests right now. So, in the midst of them, are you rushing back to this world? This world will never satisfy you. *It's like going to get in the shower using mud water.* Stop running back to your past because you think God hates you. He doesn't hate you. He loves you. He created you. He's for you. He's with you. Stop rationalizing and arguing with Him and return to Him.

How do you return?

1. Repent of your sins. Don't wait for Sunday service. Fall to your knees right now and surrender to our king Jesus.
2. Spend time with God daily.

3. Now, it's time to let God instruct you and lead you. As you acknowledge Him in all of your ways, (Proverbs 3:5) HE will direct you. So He may direct you to cut off a bad relationship, stop listening to certain music, or some other area. So, guard that heart as you go about your way. You cannot afford to listen to whoever, do whatever or live however. The Holy Spirit lives in you.

Obey quickly.

God created you and knew you before you were born. He knows you inside and out and actually mapped out a plan for your life. Trust Him.

CHAPTER 11

FORGIVENESS: THE PURPOSE BLOCKER

Ever been hurt by someone you really love? This isn't some type of "drive-by" hurt as you're driving and someone beeps their horn at you and gives you a middle finger. But this is someone you have cultivated and developed a relationship with and they HURT you. I mean really hurt you. To the point where it completely called into question your relationship with them. So, what do you do when you get wrecked like this? I mean, you love Jesus. You go to church. You try to live for Him. You said that you forgave that person. But the thought of them still makes you roll your eyes. You don't know how to let go of the **pain even though you verbally**

forgave them. They cheated on you. They abused you. They talked about you. They stole from you. They left you. They ruined your trust. They really messed up. They really broke your heart. Do they KNOW how bad they hurt you? Do they KNOW the pain they have caused in your heart? You felt like you were a good friend, wife, husband, or whatever else and you don't feel like you deserve that treatment.

I have experienced that pain. Some of you have gone through some really deep-rooted pain that I will never understand. I could never totally understand your shoes because I didn't have to walk in them. Although I have had my own share of hurt and pain-- I do know this: as Christians, we can have a different perspective in the midst of our hurt. Remember, you are NOT like this world. Your standard comes from the Lord so your RESPONSE *to the hurt must be different.* This doesn't mean that you have to run and be best friends with the girl that stole your boyfriend or the woman that crossed you the wrong way because God can reveal certain things in people as a warning to you. What do I mean by warning? As I mentioned before, everyone cannot be your friend. Some relationships are seasonal and you cannot afford to bring people that are unqualified into the next season of your life. Does this mean you hate them? No! Does this mean that you should try to open a door in that relationship because it's the "right" thing? No! It means that you should be God-led in who you surround yourself with but be QUICK to forgive them. And let me throw this in there, just because you miss a person, doesn't mean that they are supposed to be in your LIFE. We must constantly check our emotions to make sure that they are in LINE with where God is taking us.

I'm telling you that you can forgive whoever hurt you. It is possible. You can seriously, from the bottom of your heart, let it go. How? Because Christ forgave YOU. That may sound like a cliché but how is it that we are so humbled and broken before God over our own sins against Him and we want immediate freedom from whatever but the second somebody wrongs us; we hold onto that hurt. "They need to PAY for what they did, right?" **What if Christ made you pay for the way you treat Him?** You would never rest as you carried around that burden of guilt. And most of you carry that burden around. You don't think that Christ really forgave YOU so you aren't really forgiving anybody else.

When you refuse to forgive other people, it's like you

are drinking poison, praying for someone else to die. That poison is getting into your blood stream and it's eating you alive from the inside out. And all the while, you think that you are charging someone else for the way they hurt you-- but not only did they hurt you, but now they're living rent-free in your head. And most likely, that person isn't even THINKING about you or what happened. They have moved on and are going about their life and bitterness is eating you away. You see them on Facebook and they seem so happy. Deep down, seeing them happy as they only show their highlight reel makes you even more bitter. Your hurt won't change their happiness, even if they're only sharing their good moments.

How is it that you believe in forgiveness for yourself but refuse to give it to anybody else? How is it that you hold yourself to a higher standard as if forgiveness only applies to you and nobody else? How is that we want Christ more but we hate our sister or brother in Christ? How can we move on in our "ministries, callings, purpose" or whatever else if we are carrying all of this BAGGAGE?? Sis, GOD wants your HEART. So, before you run and try to start a ministry you need to run and sit at the feet of Jesus and let Him HEAL your broken heart (Psalm 147:3).

Jesus said we are to forgive others "seventy times seven" in response to Peter's question, "Lord, how many times shall I forgive my brother when he sins against me? Up to seven times?" (Matthew 18:21-22). To fully understand what Jesus was saying, we must look at the context of the whole chapter, for Jesus was speaking not only about forgiving one another, but about Christian character, both in and out of the church. If you read that chapter, Peter who is wishing to appear especially forgiving and "righteous," asked Jesus if forgiveness was to be offered seven times. The Jewish rabbis at the time taught that forgiving someone more than three times was unnecessary so Jesus had to clear it up! (Referring to Amos 1:3-13 where God forgave Israel's enemies three times, then punished them)

By offering forgiveness more than double that of the Old Testament example, Peter most likely expected extra praise from the Lord as he appeared to be forgiving AND loving. When Jesus responded that forgiveness should be offered four hundred and ninety times, which was WAY beyond that which Peter was suggesting, it must have SHOCKED the disciples who were listening. Although they had been with Jesus for some time, they were still thinking in the limited terms of the law, rather than in the unlimited terms of grace. I believe that most of us are still stuck under the terms and conditions of the law. Saying, I'm going to forgive you this many times and after that-- that's IT! After that, I will NEVER forgive you. Can you do a heart-check to see if there's anyone in your life that you've intentionally refused to forgive? Are you waiting for someone to "earn" your grace?

By saying we are to forgive those who sin against us seventy times seven, Jesus was not limiting forgiveness to 490 times-- He was saying there IS no limit to how many times we can forgive. We as Christians, with forgiving hearts, not only do we not limit the number of times WE forgive; we must continue to forgive with as much grace the thousandth time as we did the first time. WE are only capable of this type of forgiving spirit because the Spirit of God lives within us, and it is He who provides the ABILITY to offer forgiveness over and over, just as God forgives us over and over. So, it's NO longer in YOUR ability to forgive whoever hurt you! It's in CHRIST'S ABILITY. THIS is why it's important that you spend time with God and make sure that you have His perspective! You won't have God-kind-of-thinking if you fill your days with 8 hours of work, 5 hours of Facebook, 2 hours of working out and then you throw your last 10 minutes to Him as you drift off to sleep.

The Holy Spirit will HELP you! You have to stop trying to forgive everyone in your **flesh**. It just won't work. You may be reading this and think that it's impossible to forgive someone. You're RIGHT. In your own way of thinking... it IS. But through Christ, you can truly let it GO.

Let's check out a few scenarios!

1. Some of you may have been betrayed by a spouse or a friend. What do you do? How do you forgive and trust your spouse again after the hurt?

   Answer: You should learn to have amnesia in your marriage or friendships that are God-ordained. This doesn't mean you throw everything under the rug and never address everything. It just means that EVERYTHING doesn't need to be addressed every five minutes you are offended. Maybe it's not them, maybe it's you. Do you give God a chance to check you OR are you too busy popping off at the mouth? God can and WILL heal your marriage. You must adjust your mindset. You cannot just quit every time it gets hard. You will get hurt. You will have rough days. But if you get through those tests then things will get better, you'll grow closer and it will get EASIER.

Just last night, I grabbed take out from a vegan restaurant for me and Logan and headed home. As we ate our food, I started to make my husband's food as I make two separate meals. I didn't know that he was actually craving and wanted the take out, I thought he wanted a home cooked meal. I started to get upset because typically, we always ask each other if one another wants food and this time, I didn't and I assumed he wanted the food I was cooking. For my husband, he wanted to know that I thought of him to get the take out and to just give him an option. (The joys of being married to an "Acts of Service" kinda guy.)

So, I started FUMING on the inside! Maybe, it was my pregnancy hormones but I'm thinking, "You need to be GLAD I cook you a home cooked meal every single night!" How DARE HE!? As I fumed, I sensed the Holy Spirit tugging on my heart to let it go and that it wasn't worth stirring myself up and getting upset. In the future, I'll just call him to see if he wants take out. Problem solved. *Why do we complicate things in our head, meditate on them and then get upset about it?* The Bible tells us to "STIR ourselves up and encourage ourselves in the Lord." It doesn't say to stir yourself up and get mad at people that make you upset. So, stop replaying the frustrations and give them to the Lord and leave them there.

In the cases of cheating, your goal should be reconciliation. Both sides need to come together, repent, get counseling and get focused on Christ again. If your husband continually cheats on you even after the several attempts of reconciliation, he has abandoned the marriage. He has forced a divorce and left you with no option. You STILL have to forgive him as you separate and pray for him to give his life to Jesus.

2. I forgave that person BUT I still don't have good feelings towards them. What do I do?

    Answer: Forgive by faith. Some of ya'll need to, by faith, forgive someone and then just ask God to help you think good thoughts towards them. Pray for them every time their name pops up or if you see them. Whisper under your breath, "God, I pray for so and so- that they may know you and your power. May they walk in your ways and obey you in everything they do." You won't be bitter towards them long because God will really change YOUR heart. I had to do this when I felt jealousy in my heart towards a girl at my old church when I first gave my life to Christ. I knew the jealousy shouldn't be there so I prayed earnestly for her. Satan won't drop crazy suggestions in your heart about a person if you stay on your face in prayer for them.

3. My boyfriend did something to really hurt me. What do I do, do I stay?

Answer: Let's be clear- if he cheated on you or something-- I don't recommend sticking around because a ring won't change his mindset. You're obligated in a marriage to AT least attempt to make it work. In a boyfriend/girlfriend relationship you are getting an opportunity to check a person's "get down" out also known as fruit of the spirit. Again, we must always be God-led in our relationships but if your man is always lying and it's always SOMETHING and he's always trying to sleep with you and it's this or that-- a "ring" won't change him, sister. You'll be checking behind him for the rest of your LIFE. Now, this is not "formula." All of your relationships should be God-led as I said before. So, stop rationalizing, going back and forth and trying to stuff your size nine foot into a size five. It's going to be a painful journey because you will most likely never break those shoes in and your feet won't feel better until you RID yourself of that shoe and actually let God lead you to one that fits.

4. My parents hurt me. How do I get through the pain when I have to see them or a family member?

Answer: I totally understand! Whew! I know how that can be! I have been in a situation where I was hurt by a family member and first I took it to the Lord and asked the Lord to help me to forgive them. I forgave them by faith and I reached out to them to talk the situation out. I didn't feel like we were ever on the same page concerning this situation. I still felt hurt in my heart about the situation but I was determined not to give up on the person. I continued to call them, just to check up on them and prayed earnestly that God would soften and change their heart to Him. Now, it's like nothing ever happened. It's pretty amazing. Not only have I forgiven them, but now we're moving forward and are growing in our relationship. I knew that it was a relationship in my family that I couldn't just CUT off. I knew they were supposed to be in my life. There was no question.

There are some situations where you have to pull away from family members and stand up to them. In this situation, I felt like I had to stand up for what had happened. My standards and values come from Christ alone and no other place. So, that DID put a separation between me and them and it was OK because I knew that God put that wedge in between us (Matthew 10:25).

Regardless of your situation, remember this:

"Be kind and compassionate to one another, forgiving each other, just as in Christ God forgave you." **Ephesians 4:32**

CHAPTER 12

BEING CONTENT IN YOUR SEASON

If I could spell out being content it would translate as "trusting God." When you really trust God, I mean, really trust Him with all of you, you no longer focus on the situation around you. You may be feeling like, "I can't wait to get to that point in life because I ain't there Heather." I must say that being content is a daily mindset of renewing your mind. As you live for God and you trust His timing and ways, it does get easier. But if you aren't careful, you can fall back into a trap of not trusting God or being content based on what you're feeding yourself.

Feeding yourself? Yes, what are you putting in your "house?" Your house is your body and your body is the temple of the Holy Spirit. Your foundation is either going to be Him or something else. For example, my husband and I took a walk the other day and we walked by this apartment building that was being demolished. It looked TERRIBLE! Bulldozers were everywhere and I was thinking, "Gosh, what a huge undertaking!" There were piles upon piles of wood everywhere from the apartment building that used to stand there. If I were working on that project, I would have a hard time seeing the end goal because of the destruction. I thought to myself, I wonder how many people once lived in that apartment complex and the memories that were made there. I wonder if those people lived for Jesus. Then, in the midst of my thoughts, the Holy Spirit told me that THIS is what we look like when we give our lives to Jesus. It looks like a huge bulldozer came in and destroyed your entire heart. There's garbage everywhere! That garbage was on the inside of us! God wrecks our relationships, our old mindset and our lives and then, brick by brick with the RIGHT foundation, which is Him, He prepares and repairs our hearts.

It also made me wonder, how many people in the church have we thrown away that are in the middle of construction? I'm not referring to that unequally yoked boyfriend or that girl who is challenging you to disobey God in certain ways. I'm referring to that girl in your Pinky Promise group that works your nerves. I'm referring to that woman that you have to deal with on a regular basis who drives you up the wall BUT we know that person is supposed to be in our life for a reason or a season. I must say, I'm thankful that people didn't toss me away when I got hit with the bulldozer. I'm thankful for those who prayed with me, corrected me, and pushed me closer to Jesus. Remember that the only time we sever ties is when the Holy Spirit is leading us to do so.

Just like the architect has the blueprint for the project that we are working on, God has the blueprint laid out of our lives. In Jeremiah 1:5 it says, "I knew you before you were in your mother's womb and I assigned you with a purpose." God assigned Jeremiah to be a prophet, he assigned me to preach, write books and to help women under the submission of my husband. Now, God has called YOU to do something. He is looking at the blue print of your life when other people have written you off. Other people look at your destruction and roll their eyes at you and say, "You haven't changed, you look the same. Day in and day out, we drive by your 'house' and we don't see much of a difference." Then, seasons change and all the sudden they look up and God begins to put you on display. You may even look at your own huge pile of wood and life and say, "Lord, I don't see where you're taking me! This road is too hard! I don't see the blueprint of the final product and this is where weariness comes into to play that births discontentment.

Why? Because you're used to a certain level of comfort prior to Christ. And although the foundation was so messed up and confusing, you were still comfortable in your bondage. You were comfortable in your dysfunctional relationships. You were comfortable in your depression. You were comfortable in your sex. You were comfortable in your sin. You were comfortable in our pornography. You liked to please your flesh because it was selfish. Our sin nature naturally gravitates to pleasing "me" and life being all about "me." This is why when things get hard, people run back to the man, the porn, the clubs, the drugs, the drinking, the whatever else because it feels safe to them. It's like they're sitting in a pile of rubble, hoping that things will change. I want you to know that there's no profit, no fruit and no good that will come out of running back to the areas where God set you free. I repeat, **NOTHING GOOD WILL COME OUT OF PURSUING UNGODLY THINGS.**

I remember that I once had a dream when I was dating a guy I really liked. I really wanted to marry this guy for some ungodly reason. But, I always felt like his heart was with so many other women and I just didn't want to accept it. He would feed me lies and told me that he wanted to marry me one day. He would tell me that I was the perfect girl, it was just the wrong timing. I had been saved a couple years by then and I felt like God always spoke to me through my dreams in that season to confirm what He was telling me when I was awake. In the dream, I was watching the guy talk to all of these women. We were walking together and he kept flirting with all of these girls and lusting after them. Every time I would get upset, he would ignore me. After following him around to different sets of women and watching him ignore me for them, over and over again, the Lord said to me in the dream, *"this relationship has no profit. Let it go."*

When I woke up that morning, I knew that it was a God-dream (Satan likes to use dreams as well too to mess with you so you have to know the difference.) I knew that when I was awake, the Holy Spirit would convict me with this guy and when I would go to sleep, I would have dreams showing me that he wasn't right for me. So, to this day, I constantly ask myself, **"is what I'm doing profitable to bring glory to God or will I end up in destruction by pursuing this thing?**

Of course, I'm sharing my story of cutting him off in just a few words but even in cutting him off at that time it was hard. It was hard because I had built up in my head the way that my life was going to be with this man. And sometimes, we can have our plans and our ways of what we think our life is going to be like only to end up hurt, over and over again. *Is it hard to live for God and be uncomfortable for some seasons?* Absolutely! Trusting God and truly letting go of what makes you comfortable is HARD. I'm sure that apartment building that I saw had been up for years and maybe someone lived there that entire time. I'm sure they were comfortable with where they lived and didn't want to move. But then, the building sold and change had to come, so, they had to get up and move.

Another story, every day, I drive by this huge building that is under construction and it says, "To be completed in April of 2014." And my heart breaks for the investor because

I'm sure it's an eye-sore to him to see a project not completed, money wasted and the sign still stating that he's over a year late on his project. You see, God has dates set for you but, if you constantly disobey Him, ignore Him and try to live your own life then your "due" dates are going to pass. As we read in Ecclesiastes 3 above there's a SEASON under the sun for everything. I'm pretty sure that Saul missed out on a lot of things because of his disobedience to the Lord and I don't want that to be your story. Each season in your life is truly prepping you for the next so you have to let God prep you. Let Him burn out of you the things that aren't like Him! We must learn to trust Him through this journey.

I know that it is hard to trust God at times. I know that you have your good days and then you have some really rough days where you're thinking, Lord, how long before this or that? How long before my breakthrough? How long will I have to trust you to rebuild my foundation? How long before I get married? How long before I will have children? How long before I will be debt free? I've learned that I can't focus on "this or that" or what I think I'm lacking. My focus must be on the Lord alone because *if I'm content with just Him, then He won't bring things into my life so that I can make those things my idols*. I've said this over and over again in my past three books, that anything you have to have in order to be satisfied will be used against you by the enemy. Satan will have a field day in your life because you think those things will satisfy you and only God can truly fill those voids on the inside of your heart. I said that only GOD can fill those voids in your heart. No handbag, no man, no person, not thing, no job, no sex, no temporary thing on this earth can ever take the place of God. This is why we must learn to be content in our current state in life.

> *Not that I was ever in need, for I have learned how to be content with whatever I have. I know how to live on almost nothing or with everything. I have learned the secret of living in every situation, whether it is with a full stomach or empty, with plenty or little. For I can do everything through Christ, who gives me strength.*
> **Philippians 4:11-13 NLT**

So, the secret to being married or not is Christ. The secret to not getting that job or getting it is in Christ. The secret to not having a car or having a car is Christ. The secret to eating eggs for dinner or steak for dinner is Christ. Now, insert your situation.

I've learned that even if I get my steak dinner (example only as I'm a vegetarian ;)) it still won't make me happy. **An event, meeting a certain person or having children will definitely add to your life but it cannot replace our relationship with Jesus.** One day, it's almost like the blinders fell off of my eyes and the Lord showed me that adding anything else to my plate will only reveal who I really am on the inside. Getting married only showed me my selfishness. Having a child only showed me how impatient I can be. Your issues will be amplified one hundred times as you enter different seasons. So, remember that external things will NEVER satisfy you and you will keep coming up empty." Sis, you have got to stop trying to solve internal issues with external events.

So, whether it happens or not, you are content in Christ. Isn't that a powerful statement? You may have read that scripture a million times but maybe it hasn't really become real in your heart. We must come to a place in our walk where we say, "Lord, whether it happens or not, you are my portion, you are my strength, you are my joy. I TRUST you as a good Father to provide what I NEED in due season." It's a dangerous prayer but it shows that your heart is truly surrendered to Him.

I remember getting tested with my family members on Christmas day back in 2008 when I was single and focused on the Lord. All of my family wanted to know, why I was 26, single, with a good job, a degree, loved Jesus and couldn't "get a man." I explained to them that it wasn't about getting a man, I could get any ole man but I just knew God called me to something great. I knew that I had to have a standard and because He hadn't shown me any potential men, I was going to remain by myself. I told the Lord that I could be single for the next ten years and be satisfied because He was truly all I needed. Then, nine days later, I met my now husband. Is this a "formula" to tell you that you're going to get a man, get pregnant, get a job, get whatever in nine days? Not at all! But what I am saying, is that I was focused and intentional about developing my relationship with Jesus and I refused to let discontentment steal my joy.

Do I "have" everything I want? **Gosh, that's no longer my focus.** It can't be your focus either. Just wake up, take each day, day by day and give your days the Lord. I used to focus on what I didn't have and then those things became amplified in my heart. If you stare at something long enough, that thing will be all you can see. And some of us *keep* staring at other people's relationships, other people's ministries, other people's success, other peoples this or that. We've taken our eyes off of Christ and we have put them on humans. This is one of the many dangers of social media. We may find some value in simply getting off of social media for a few weeks until we have the proper mindset towards it.

When I first opened up my social media accounts, I wanted to encourage people and tell them about Jesus. I don't follow a bunch of "rappers or celebrities." I'm not judging people who do, but I have no reason to follow their lives because I find that if I follow them and they are without Christ then without even realizing it, I could compare my life to theirs. Well, look at their clothes, their life, they seem so happy, look at their money, I wish I had what they had.

Honey, those things are temporary! Who cares? God has you on a certain journey and it's vital that you stay the course. You have to guard your heart and you cannot afford to be following people and allowing for their words and lifestyle to penetrate your heart. Mark my words, it's that deep.

How can we change this mindset? Our focus must

shift from what we think we need, to the cross. So, if that door opens or not, it doesn't matter. Our focus was never on that door opening, it's in Christ, so, if the door opens, great! If not, it wasn't supposed to open and I continue to trust Him.

I recall this past week where we were interviewing to host a TV show (that actually lined up with our standards) on one of the largest TV networks on TV. To make a long story short, we didn't get the job because we were set to give birth to our daughter around the time of recording the show. Was I upset? No. God surly wasn't surprised that I was giving birth at the time of the show. He makes no mistakes and if it was for me, it would have never been taken from me. My heart has changed. I know that the plans that God has for me are good. (Jeremiah 29:11) So, it wasn't good that I walked through that door.

Did this mindset happen all of the sudden? No, it was a gradual journey. Christ came and changed our hearts. He convicted us of our sin and the Holy Spirit came in, destroyed the sin and started the real healing process. So, as the foundation is being laid, it can be pretty painful. It can be hard. It can be frustrating. Things can seem slow. God won't allow certain bricks to be laid from your past. It's like we take that bulldozer of a mess that we discussed earlier in this chapter and we leave the mess there while trying to build a new foundation. That foundation won't stand on the pile of rubble left over from the demolition! If you keep building over a foundation that hasn't been wiped clean by the Holy Spirit, you are going to end up going around the same mountain in your life again. You will keep attracting those crazy men, you will continue in an unhappy marriage, you will continue to blame everybody else for what has happened to you. It's time to go before the Lord and give Him everything—every hurt, every pain every ounce of discontentment, every fear and anything else that may hinder us in our walk.

In the midst of these things happening, it can seem almost like you are forgotten but you must stay faithful to the Lord and keep living for Him. You cannot stop, you cannot quit, you cannot run back to the vomit that the Lord has freed you from! There's NO profit there! One day, your house will stand tall and beautiful with the RIGHT foundation. Each day, when you wake up and spend that time with God and choose Him, a beautiful brick is being laid. Each time people bash you and you respond lovingly, a beautiful new brick is being laid. Each time you forgive people that hurt you, another brick is laid. So then, when the attacks and the winds of this world come, it won't be able to knock your house down.

"The rain came down, the streams rose, and the winds blew and beat against that house; yet it did not fall, because it had its foundation on the rock."
Matthew 7:25

Jesus is preparing you for ETERNITY. This life is so much bigger than these temporary things. So, we must practice to be content RIGHT where we are in life. An event won't change a discontent heart so even with that child you prayed for, you still may find yourself unhappy. Even with that husband you believed God for, you will still find that he isn't the source of your joy. Even moving to that new location, you will find ways to be unhappy. Being content is a heart issue. Your contentment proves who you trust.

Who do you trust?

CHAPTER 13

THE FINAL MARRIAGE

Try to imagine this if you can! You've finally met the man of your dreams and you find out that he is going to skip proposing to you all together but instead, he will "capture" you, taking you away for your wedding day and HE has made all the plans! How many of you would actually be OK with your now boyfriend or even now husband planning your entire wedding and you not even knowing the day or time? Well, that's exactly what happened in Jewish custom. The bride didn't know the day or the hour to when her groom would come to marry her. There's no engagement photos or anything, when they meet their groom, they sign a contract stating that they will get married and that first meeting is considered the beginning of the "engaged" time period.

Then, your groom places a veil on your head that signifies that you are taken. You are to wear that veil everywhere you go until your wedding day. Again, you don't know the time or hour to when you will need to be prepared, so, you have to constantly be ready for the wedding day. Same goes for our final marriage to Christ. Your groom (Christ) can come at any time, even in the middle of the night or at midnight. Therefore, we have to be ready at all times.

> "Then the Kingdom of Heaven will be like ten bridesmaids who took their lamps and went to meet the bridegroom. Five of them were foolish, and five were wise. **The** five who were foolish didn't take enough olive oil for their lamps, but the other five were wise enough to take along extra oil. When the bridegroom was delayed, they all became drowsy and fell asleep. "At midnight they were roused by the shout, 'Look, the bridegroom is coming! Come out and meet him!'" **Matthew 25:1-6**

It's clear that the wedding is unexpected and at a moment's notice. So, what are you doing in the midst of your idle time? Do you get bored or become desensitized to living for God because you don't think he's coming anymore? Or maybe, you think you have time to prepare for your marriage. Maybe, you are lonely and you keep running back to your past. Or maybe you're just so sick and tired of your husband that your heart is hardened towards him. You've pretty much turned away from God all together and your heart is hardened towards Him. So, which bridesmaid are you? Is your lamp full? If Christ comes at midnight, will you be able to see the path in front of you with the lamp from your oil or will it be dark? Will you trip and fall because you are absolutely shocked that everything you've heard about God is real? This walk is REAL! Heaven and hell is real. Angels are real. Demons are real. Satan is real. We should live with the mindset that Jesus can return for us at any moment.

As a single, I feared going to bed with a random little boyfriend and waking up standing before Jesus. It got to a point where it just wasn't worth my salvation. Salvation? Heather, once saved always saved, right? No, my sister. You see, if you simply utter a few words and cry, it doesn't make you saved. Salvation is a lifestyle of waking up and choosing God every single day of your life. As you CHOOSE to live for Him, He leads and guides your life. That leading and guiding includes cutting off bad relationships, lifestyles, addictions and anything that is hindering your fellowship with Him. If we say that we love God, then our lives must show it. I said, our lives must display this love that we have for Him. The truth is, you were most likely never converted so you were never saved in the first place. There's a difference in our pursuit. Christians pursue Jesus, others pursue sin.

> And we can be sure that we know him if we obey his commandments. If someone claims, "I know God," but doesn't obey God's commandments, that person is a liar and is not living in the truth. But those who obey God's word truly show how completely they love him. That is how we know we are living in him. Those who say they live in God should live their lives as Jesus did. **1 John 2:3-6**

Let's take a moment and answer this question: **What are God's commandments?**

> "Teacher, which is the greatest commandment in the Law?" Jesus replied: "Love the Lord your God with all your heart and with all your soul and with all your mind. This is the first and greatest commandment. And the second is like it: Love your neighbor as yourself. All the Law and the Prophets hang on these two commandments.
> **Matthew 22:36-40 NLT**

So, when we love God first, we won't place anybody else over Him. When we love God, we will submit to our husbands as unto the Lord. When we love God, we won't sleep around. When we love God, we will capture those stupid thoughts that oppose God and make them submit to God's word. When we love God, we will be intentional about honoring Him in every way. When we love God, we will give our nasty attitudes to Him. When we love God, we won't be lazy in our walk, letting negative influences plant seeds in our heart. We will guard our hearts from foolishness and truly love God.

That means, if we say that we love God but we continue to intentionally sin, then we don't really love God. We say that we do, but our life's decisions prove who we belong to.

You have to understand that your bridegroom has paid the price for you by saving you. He came down to the earth to die for your sins and paid the "dowry" for your life. Like the women in the Old Testament used to wear veils, we should all walk around with an invisible veil, showing that we belong to Christ. We are covered, we are hidden, we are protected and we show this world that we belong to Jesus and only He paid the price for us. His precious blood was shed for you because no other god came down to this earth to reconcile you back to God. Then it's up to your groom, Jesus, to identify that you belong to Him. He identifies those who belong to Him based on who has the Holy Spirit living in them. He knows His bride.

As God searches the earth, He can easily see who belongs to Him and who does not because we are spirits that live in a body and we possess a soul (mind, will and emotions.) The veil worn by us brides should say, "I'm consecrated, set-apart and I am LOYAL to my groom! I don't serve any other god. I belong to King Jesus! This is why we don't serve Muhammad, Buddha or any other god. Only Jesus Christ came to the earth, lived a sinless life and died for your sins. Now, He is the door that reconciles us back to God. He left the earth but He didn't leave us alone. He sent the Holy Spirit to the earth to lead and guide our paths.

The Holy Spirit cannot be manipulated and we cannot live for this world, dressing up on the outside and saying that we belong to Jesus. The proof will be on your wedding night and if you are prepared to meet your groom. Our prayer should be from Ezekiel 36:26 *"And I will give you a new heart, and I will put a new spirit in you. I will take out your stony, stubborn heart and give you a tender, responsive heart."*

When Jesus returns for His bride (us) He will come with a shout.

Matthew 25:6 says that "at midnight they were roused by the shout, 'Look, the bridegroom is coming! Come out and meet him!'" Paul describes what the return of the groom will be like:

> *And with the blowing of a trumpet. For the Lord himself will come down from heaven, with a loud command, with the voice of the archangel and with the trumpet call of God, and the dead in Christ will rise first. After that, we who are still alive and are left will be caught up together with them in the clouds to meet the Lord in the air. And so we will be with the Lord forever. Therefore encourage one another with these words.* **1 Thessalonians 4:16-18**

The Greek term meaning **"caught up"** is *harpazo*, means to seize suddenly or snatch. In Latin the word is *rapio*, is used to describe the same idea—to seize and carry away. It is from this Latin word that the term "rapture" comes. When Jesus returns those of you who are read for the wedding will be raptured, will be caught up, seized and carried away by the groom.

I think that at times we view weddings as just saying

vows and "walking down the aisle" but THIS is the final wedding. When the Lord returns, He's already said His vows to us and now, we will be reunited with Him! What a beautiful day that will be!

I did some studying on the tribulation period and I found that there are a lot of viewpoints on what is going to happen. Let me sum them up here.

1. **Post-tribulation**: believers are raptured at the end of the tribulation period, when Christ returns in judgment (cf. Revelation 19). We are here, waiting for Christ to return.

2. **Pre-wrath**: believers are caught up somewhere between the sixth and seventh seals described in Revelation.

3. **Mid-tribulation**: living believers are taken in the middle of the tribulation period.

4. **Partial rapture**: only faithful believers are taken to be with Christ at the beginning of the tribulation, with unfaithful Christians being left to endure it.

5. **Pre-tribulation**: believers are caught up to be with Christ before the tribulation begins.

I say all this to say that Jesus is returning. He is coming back soon! Will you be like the foolish bridesmaids found in Matthew 25?

"Then the Kingdom of Heaven will be like ten bridesmaids who took their lamps and went to meet the bridegroom. Five of them were foolish, and five were wise. The five who were foolish didn't take enough olive oil for their lamps, but the other five were wise enough to take along extra oil. When the bridegroom was delayed, they all became drowsy and fell asleep.

*"At midnight they were roused by the shout, 'Look, the bridegroom is coming! Come out and meet him! "All the bridesmaids got up and prepared their lamps. Then the five foolish ones asked the others, 'Please give us some of your oil because our lamps are going out." But the others replied, 'We don't have enough for all of us. Go to a shop and buy some for yourselves." But while they were gone to buy oil, the bridegroom came. Then those who were ready went in with him to the marriage feast, and the door was locked. Later, when the other five bridesmaids returned, they stood outside, calling, 'Lord! Lord! Open the door for us!' "But he called back, 'Believe me, I don't know you!' "So you, too, must keep watch! For you do not know the day or hour of my return. **Matthew 25:1-13 NLT***

The oil signifies the Holy Spirit (Isaiah 61:1) and there are a lot of churches all over the world with empty lamps. There's no mention of the Holy Spirit in some churches nor is the Word of God faithfully preached. There are empty lamps lying around everywhere and they will continue to hold services long after the Rapture. People that are lukewarm for God will say, "Please give us the Holy Spirit so we can see the path that leads to the Lord!" You see, what they don't understand is that the Holy Spirit cannot be bought, manipulated or fabricated. Either He lives IN you or He does not live in you. We must have the Holy Spirit and be true believers in Jesus in order to leave this earth with Him. When we get saved and give our lives to Jesus, what we cannot see is the Holy Spirit as he enters and LIVES IN us. HE is the identifier when Jesus returns for His bride! Don't be like the foolish bride that runs out of oil because she never truly abided in Christ.

When Jesus returns for us, we will then enter into the honeymoon period. It's not your typical honeymoon of total bliss because it's when us brides will remove our veils and reveal all of our secrets. We will be spiritual creatures when we meet Christ so we will be "changed" and our Groom will examine our spiritual secrets.

> *"For no one can lay any foundation other than the one we already have—Jesus Christ. Anyone who builds on that foundation may use a variety of materials—gold, silver, jewels, wood, hay, or straw. But on the judgment day, fire will reveal what kind of work each builder has done. The fire will show if a person's work has any value. But if the work is burned up, the builder will suffer great loss. The builder will be saved, but like someone barely escaping through a wall of flames.*
> **1 Corinthians 3:11-13 NLT**

So, on your honeymoon, every deed, every thought, every work, every action, every word will have to pass through the fire. The fire will PROVE if what you were doing was for you or for God. The beauty in this is that Jesus cannot allow works to enter into His kingdom that aren't like Him so He HAS to burn those things out of you that aren't like Him. Heaven has no sin, no crazy mindsets, thoughts, wrong motives or works. Thank God for His grace and mercy!

As you stand there on your honeymoon, on judgment day, naked before the Lord, what will pass through the fire? Will you stand confidently and boldly, knowing that you intentionally obeyed the Lord or will it be a day of shame for you as you watch every gossiping word you spoke, every hateful email you sent, every person you hurt, every sin you pursued?

So, is God finding you in position or are you constantly running from Him? Remember that He loves you so much that He gives you free will. Free will to choose Him or another god and although you may not bow down and worship money, that loser boyfriend, your busy schedule or whatever else, if it's causing your lamps to become empty, then it's a distraction!

So, mark this day that you read these words. **It's time to let go of anything or anyone that is hindering your walk with the Lord.** Jesus is returning for you. You have to cut it off. You have to let it go! Jesus came as your groom and paid the "dowry" for you by dying for your sins! He paid the price for you! No other person, job, or whatever else paid this cost! He's jealous for you because you belong to Him and you are choosing other things and other people. And one day, you will be judged on these things.

One day, you will actually meet Jesus face-to-face. You will look at Him in His eyes and what will you say? Will you fall onto your face in regret for the life you pretended to live or will you fall on your face as He picks you up and says, "Well done my faithful daughter." Since we know that this life is but a vapor and that not even tomorrow is promised, **we have to stop getting caught up in this earth.** You cannot take all your stuff, your man or your job with you to heaven. You will stand before Jesus, the One who died for you and be held accountable for the decisions that you made in this physical body. So, from this point forward, **let's live like tomorrow is our wedding day.** Since we don't know the hour or the day of His return, let's walk around in our veil, covered by the blood of Jesus, set apart and chosen by the Holy Spirit to represent Him on this earth.